Berlitz

Rhodes

Front c
occupie

Right: o
frame t
Town's

TOP 10 ATTRACTIONS

Rhodes New Town • The main surprise here is the whimsical Italian architecture in a variety of 1920s and 1930s styles *(page 44)*

Líndos • A collection of old sea captains' mansions sit beneath the towering Acropolis with its ancient Temple of Athena *(page 56)*

Petaloúdes • The Valley of the Butterflies offers an idyllic escape from the summer heat and sightings of rare Jersey tiger moths *(page 65)*

Sými Island • Deservedly the most popular day-trip destination from Rhodes, the port is a stunning tableau of preserved Neoclassical mansions *(page 78)*

Palace of the Grand Masters • The imposing centrepiece of Rhodes Old Town houses two excellent museums with some fascinating ancient and medieval exhibits *(page 35)*

Kameiros • The most scenic and untouched of the island's ancient sites *(page 67)*

Thárri Monastery • The 14th- and 15th-century frescoes in the church are the most noteworthy on Rhodes *(page 60)*

Tsambíka Bay • Soft golden sand meets clear sparkling water at this lovely beach *(page 54)*

Kritiniá Castle • Though a ruined shell, this fort offers great views of the western islets *(page 70)*

Street of the Knights • This 14th-century street in Rhodes Old Town is so atmospheric that it is frequently used as a film location *(page 32)*

CONTENTS

37

77

22

INTRODUCTION

I t is impossible not to feel the weight of history when you arrive in Rhodes. The granite of Dorian settlements, marble of Classical sites and sandstone of medieval churches and castles are all tangible legacies of a long historical timeline. However, to think that Rhodes is only of interest to archaeology buffs would be a mistake. With long, hot summer days, a balmy sea lapping numerous beaches, and lots to do, the island is a holidaymakers' paradise.

Rhodes is the largest island in the Dodecanese, an archipelago lying in the southeastern Aegean Sea between Greece and Turkey. Originally made up of 12 major islands (*dódeka nisiá* means '12 islands' in Greek) that formed an alliance against Ottoman and Italian repression early in the 20th century, the group is now an administrative region of Greece comprising several dozen islands and islets, though only 22 have a permanent population.

A Turbulent History

The ebb and flow of history has washed over Rhodes, with periods of influence and great wealth alternating with centuries as a backwater. Lying only 10 nautical miles from the Asia Minor coastline, Rhodes was an important stepping-stone on the trade routes between east and west throughout Classical, Hellenistic and Roman times. The Rhodians were adept at commerce and cultivated trading partners around the Mediterranean, bringing sustained prosperity to the island. Traces of this flourishing culture can be seen at the ruins of their three main city-states – Lindos, Kameiros and Ialysos.

Socrates Street in Rhodes Old Town

After the Roman Empire disintegrated, this strategically important territory became a lightly defended outpost of Byzantium, left to the mercy of raiding pirates and barbarian tribes. Its population lived in fear until the early 14th century, when it became home to the Order of the Knights Hospitaller of St John, recently ousted from the Holy Land by Muslim forces. The Knights changed the island's landscape irrevocably, undertaking a huge building programme that created some of the strongest fortifications in Europe. Rhodes Old Town still stands as a monument to their wealth, steadfastness and faith; the entire citadel has been designated a World Heritage site.

Rhodes' wild-flower meadows are at their finest in spring

The influence of the island's subsequent rulers can also be seen. When Ottoman Turkish forces drove the Knights out and took up residence in 1522, they created a comfortable Islamic outpost, complete with carved marble fountains, delicate wooden-balconied windows, elegant minarets and majestic mosque domes. The Italians, who supplanted the Turks just before World War I, invested vast sums of money, creating a new administrative centre in Rhodes New Town, restoring many historic buildings and directing their archaeologists' attention to the ancient sites.

Traditional Island Life

Despite these various over-lords, the basic way of life for the ordinary Rhodian people, governed by seasons of planting, tending and harvesting, changed little over 5,000 years. Since the Bronze Age the seas have provided abundant food, the long summers have brought forth crops of grain, and well-established olive trees and vines have borne fruit. The island's hillsides have always pro-duced good grazing for live-stock, and donkeys and mules provided a reliable means of transport.

Women at worship

Women have traditionally formed the majority of the congregation, praying on behalf of fathers, husbands and sons off diving for sponges or away at sea in merchant fleets.

From the early Christian era onwards the fabric of life was sustained by religion. The Orthodox Church became a cornerstone of Greek identity long before the modern state emerged in 1832. In times of natural disaster, war, disease and occupation, the church served as a place of refuge and solace, both physically and spiritually. Across Rhodes, small whitewashed churches each house an icon-screen with several icons and lit candles or oil-lamps; some also have incredible frescoes adorning their domes and walls.

Yet island life has seen more change in the last forty years than in the previous thousand. Rhodes is now 'invaded' by up to 1 million people annually, creating both fantastic opportunities and great pressures for the island and its people. Over half of the island population now lives in Rhodes

Traces of the Ottomans can still be seen

Town, taking advantage of the many amenities in this university town and provincial capital. But despite the growth of the main town and tourist resorts, rural lifestyles still exist in the far south and interior of the island. Here, shepherds and their flocks still rest under the shade of pine trees, and grapes ripen slowly on low-growing vines on the slopes above the wine villages.

Although Rhodes has given up many of its traditional ways, some things haven't changed. Life still revolves around the family, and each new addition is proudly shown off at the evening stroll *(vólta)*. Children play happily and safely in the streets, watched over by doting grandparents. A Greek gathering of family and friends would not be complete without ardent debate. After all, this was the country that invented democratic decision-making through discussion; if the conversation gets a bit heated then so much the better. The sound of the Greek language seems to be made for animated argument – and seldom does anyone go home bearing a grudge.

Rhodes of the Resorts

The major resorts are international territory, with foreign-language restaurant signs and menus along with daily English-language newspapers, imported beers and sports bars with satellite broadcasts. Since most hotel and tourism workers speak English, it can be easy to forget that you are in Greece if you choose not to venture out of your resort.

Those who do decide to explore the island will discover that Rhodian hospitality is both genuine and refreshing. A pocketful of Greek phrases used at the taverna will earn you honest appreciation and produce smiles and approving nods from the older gentlemen enjoying a leisurely lunch or dinner.

Tourism has brought wealth and security, and the current generation expects more than the precarious lives experienced by their parents and grandparents. As incomes have risen, farmers have replaced their trusty donkeys with trucks; many have given up their trade altogether to open a bar or car-rental office. You'll find that some fishermen now use their boats to ferry tourists to nearby beaches rather than to catch fish.

Nowadays, mobile phones are heard far more frequently than the haunting cadences of the *bouzoúki*, and only

The perfect golden sands of Tsambíka Bay

Tourists flood the streets of Líndos in high season

old-timers have leisure to linger over a game of backgammon at the *kafenío* while the younger men strive to impress the girls with new fast cars or motorbikes. There is a sophistication here not found in most other Aegean towns – a casino, a summer film festival, modern boutiques selling all the latest designer wear, and teenage girls out on the town without the chaperone that was considered an absolute necessity only a generation ago.

Rhodes has grasped with both hands the opportunity of catering for the modern worshippers of the sun god Helios, and it provides an excellent product for its visitors. Good transport connections, a plethora of eateries, bars and nightclubs and a relaxed lifestyle all contribute to a great holiday experience. Spring or autumn are ideal times for clambering up ruins, castles or the odd hiking trail, while in summer you can simply take in some rays or enjoy a range of watersports, golf, or the latest hair-raising amusement ride. No matter what time of year, the world-class architectural showcases of Rhodes Old Town and Líndos are worth a visit. Whatever your interests, there is bound to be something on Rhodes to suit you. Perhaps that's why so many people keep coming back for more.

A BRIEF HISTORY

Few traces remain of Rhodes' first inhabitants, a rugged Anatolian people who could fashion simple tools and pottery. During the Middle Bronze Age (2500–1500BC), Carians from Asia Minor and Phoenicians from Lebanon settled on the island before moving west to Crete. Traffic was two-way – Minoan merchants from Crete set up shop in Rhodes, which at the time was part of a lucrative trading network that included Egypt and the Levant. Around 1450BC a major natural disaster caused by the eruption and collapse of a volcano on ancient Thera (now Santoríni) brought about the destruction of Minoan society.

Mycenaeans from the Greek mainland soon occupied both Crete and Rhodes. These seafaring warriors are still famous for the legendary war they waged against the Trojans around 1220BC, as recounted in Homer's *Iliad*. According to Homer, 'nine ships of the arrogant Rhodians' sailed in Agamemnon's 1,000-strong fleet. The 10-year war ended with the destruction of Troy, but it also left the exhausted conquerors vulnerable to attack. The 'Sea Peoples' appeared from beyond the Black Sea around 1150BC, devastating all empires in their path. Many Greeks emigrated from the mainland to Rhodes. Over time, the fusion of the 'Sea Peoples' with the area's previous inhabitants resulted in the Classical Greek civilisation.

The Rhodian City-States

The first major settlements on Rhodes were the city-states of Lindos, Kameiros and Ialysos (named after the mythical grandsons of the sun god Helios), which reached their

Heavenly gift

According to legend the sun god Helios gave the island as a gift to his favourite nymph, Rodon, who in turn gave her name to the place. Others claim that the word is a corruption of *rodi*, 'pomegranate' in Greek.

zenith in the 1st millennium BC. By 700BC, the three city-states, together with the Asia Minor ports of Halikarnassos (now Bodrum) and Knidos, and the island of Kos, had set up a six-city trading league, the Dorian Hexapolis. Each city minted its own coins (money had just been invented in Asia Minor), and Lindian ships sailed as far as the western Mediterranean.

In the 5th century BC, a large force dispatched by the king of Persia, Darius, reached the Aegean. The city-states of mainland Greece – Athens and Sparta – stood in the way of this invasion. Anticipating a Greek defeat, Rhodes and many neighbouring islands joined forces with the Persians, but the tide turned at the land battle of Marathon in 490BC. When the Greeks sank the fleet of Darius' son, Xerxes, at the epic naval battle of Salamis 10 years later, there were around 40 Rhodian ships among the victims. The Greeks exacted swift retribution on those islands allied with the defeated enemy.

The Delian League was founded soon afterwards, under the leadership of Athens, as an attempt to bring unity and security to the Greek city- and island-states, and Rhodes became a taxpaying member. This league did much to ensure economic and political strength for the region over the coming centuries.

The Founding of Rhodes Town

Due to its strategic position on vital trade routes in the eastern Mediterranean, Rhodes grew in importance as a maritime power and financial centre. By 408BC, the volume of trade and shipping had become too much for the island's three existing ports to handle. By the mutual consent of the three existing city-states, the new port of Rhodes was founded at a spot on the northern tip of the island with three natural harbours. The city's gridiron street plan was laid out by the famous architect Hippodamos of Miletos, and many of today's thoroughfares still follow their predecessors. The new city prospered, while Ialysos and Kameiros declined to become

The Temple of Athena Lindia at Lindos

little more than religious cult centres – though Lindos remained important thanks to its two well-protected ports.

When Alexander the Great rose to power, Rhodes allied itself with the Macedonian and prospered as part of his empire, in particular benefiting from trade concessions with Egypt. After the great leader's death in 323BC, Rhodes refused to join an expedition by his successor, Antigonos, against Ptolemy I, the Macedonian general who had become the king of Egypt.

As a result Antigonos' son Demetrios Polyorketes, 'Besieger of Many Cities', led one of the most celebrated campaigns of ancient times against Rhodes in 305BC. Demetrios had an army of 40,000 troops and a fleet of over 200 ships with which to blockade the city. Against this the Rhodians could only muster about 25,000 soldiers, most of them foreign mercenaries or local slaves promised their freedom in the event of victory. After unsuccessful attacks on the harbour walls, Demetrios deployed the Helepolis, an ingenious,

125-tonne siege machine nine storeys high and 27m (90ft) wide at the base. Sheathed in leather and heavy-gauge bronze, it was propelled on oaken wheels by a crew of 3,400 people up against the landward ramparts of the city, firing missiles and landing invading troops. In response, Rhodian engineers tunnelled under the walls and undermined the path of the machine, causing it to founder.

After nearly a year's siege, the hostilities ended in a truce that confirmed Rhodes' independence, but required the island to assist any Macedonian military efforts not directed against Ptolemy. Demetrios handed over the remains of his siege engine to the Rhodians, on condition that they sell it and build a commemorative monument from the proceeds. Thus was born the famous Colossus, one of the Seven Wonders of the Ancient World.

A World Wonder

Contrary to popular belief, the Colossus of Rhodes did not straddle the entrance to Mandráki Harbour – its 20 tonnes of bronze would have sunk immediately into the soft seabed. More credible theories place this statue of the sun god Helios near the Palace of the Grand Masters.

It took sculptor Khares of Lindos 12 years to cast the 35m (114ft) Colossus – each finger was supposedly the size of a man. Khares committed suicide after discovering an apparently critical design flaw, and the work was finished by his disciple Lakhes. During an earthquake less than 70 years after its completion, the Colossus cracked at the knees and crashed to the ground – perhaps vindicating Khares' remorse.

The Rhodians consulted the Delphic Oracle, which warned them not to restore the statue. The crumpled image lay where it had fallen for nearly 900 years until AD653, when Arab pirates sacked Rhodes and sold off the bronze as scrap to a Jewish merchant from Syria who, legend says, needed 900 camels to carry it off.

Hellenistic Heyday, Roman Dominance

At the peak of its power, and with a population slightly more than today's 110,000, Rhodes enjoyed a golden age during the 3rd century BC. The island won fame as a cultural and intellectual centre, with its renowned school of rhetoric founded in 342BC by the Athenian Aeskhines. Rhodian artists and craftsmen enjoyed a privileged social standing and were highly regarded throughout the area. When the Colossus was top-

The Colossus never actually straddled Mandráki Harbour

pled by an earthquake in 227BC, the rest of the city was destroyed too, but such was its prestige in the Hellenistic world that ample financial and technical help was sent to rebuild it.

Early in the 2nd century BC, Rhodes became an important ally of the Romans, but in 166BC angered them by siding with Perseus of Macedonia. As punishment, Rome declared the island of Delos a free port, thus depriving Rhodes of a substantial income from port duties. The Rhodians hastily renewed their alliance with Rome, but soon became embroiled in the Roman civil wars. Rhodes supported Pompey against Julius Caesar, but after his victory, Caesar forgave them. Then Cassius and Brutus, Caesar's assassins, demanded Rhodian help in their war against the Senate. When this was refused, Cassius conquered and sacked Rhodes. He dispatched 3,000 statues to Rome, leaving nothing but *The Sun* – a famous sculpture of Helios' chariot by Lysippos, too heavy to remove. Almost all of this precious art was destroyed when Rome burned in AD64.

Crusaders and Knights

Christianity took root during the 1st century AD, aided by St Paul, who visited the island some 25 years after the Crucifixion. However, the new religion did not bring divine protection – Rhodes city was shattered by earthquakes in 155, 178 and 515. Much weakened, it was plundered by Goths in 263, and overrun by the Persians and Arabs in the 7th century and by the Seljuks in the 9th century. Although nominally part of the Byzantine Empire, Rhodes was a poorly defended backwater, unceasingly harassed by pirates.

Thárri Monastery dates from the 9th century

By the 11th century, followers of Muhammad had conquered Jerusalem, Islamised Persia and North Africa, converted the Turks and occupied much of Spain's territory. They represented a serious challenge to Christianity and the security of Europe. During this period Rhodes' ties with western Europe were strengthened by trade and the passage of the first crusaders on their way east to Jerusalem in 1097. In 1191, Richard the Lionheart and Philippe Auguste of France landed in Rhodes to recruit crusaders. However, despite winning some significant gains in the interim period, by 1291 the crusaders had relinquished their foothold in the Holy Land.

Among the retreating Christians were the Knights of the Order of St John, founded in Jerusalem around 1100 to offer medical assistance to ailing pilgrims. During the Crusades, these Knights Hospitaller became increasingly militaristic, learning the value of both pitched battles and fortifications. They initially settled on Cyprus, but moved to Rhodes in

1306, thinking that it would make a better stronghold. Over the next three years they wrested control of the island from Genoese and Venetian adventurers and the Byzantine Empire. By 1309 the Knights were well entrenched, and over the next 213 years they overhauled the flimsy Byzantine defences of the city in successive phases.

Beyond the city, the Knights relied on a network of nearly 30 fortresses scattered across Rhodes, on smaller nearby islands, and at Bodrum on the Anatolian mainland. The Knights were formidable warriors, and aided by Rhodian supporters they repelled attacks by the Sultan of Egypt in 1440 and 1444. In 1480 they also brilliantly outmanoeuvred the massed forces of Ottoman Sultan Mehmet II.

Ottoman forces gather outside the walls of Rhodes in 1480

The Ottoman Conquest

Nonetheless, Ottoman naval power was growing in the eastern Mediterranean, and Rhodes was a perennial concern. On 26 June 1522 Süleyman the Magnificent's fleet appeared just off the island's north tip. Shuttling back and forth from the Turkish mainland, 200 ships carried 200,000 soldiers, sappers, sailors, equipment, food and supplies, and by 9 July the city was under siege.

Over the next few months, the Ottomans lost almost 100,000 men in their attempt

Süleyman the Magnificent

to take the fortified city. They were on the verge of giving up in late September when a traitor, Grand Chancellor Andrea d'Amaral, revealed that the Christians were also at the limits of their resolve. The Ottomans renewed their attacks all through October and November, breaching the walls at several spots and penetrating the town. On 10 December the Knights, urged on in part by the civilians who hoped to emerge alive, ran up the white flag, and 10 days later a formal surrender was signed between the Knights' Grand Master and Süleyman. Its terms were generous: on 1 January 1523 the 180 surviving Knights were allowed to sail away with honour and their arms, taking with them 5,000 Christians, plus whatever treasures and religious relics the Ottomans had not already plundered. Within seven years they established a new base on the island of Malta.

For nearly four centuries, until 1912, Rhodes remained a sleepy Ottoman provincial possession. Several large mosques and some baths were built, but often Christian churches were converted to Islamic use. The Palace of the Grand Masters became a barn, and the inns of the Knights served as barracks or the dwellings of governors. Only Muslims and Jews were allowed to live in the walled city; at sunset, any Greeks working there had to leave for their homes in the *marásia*, or surrounding suburbs, which had been established outside the city walls. This segregation ensured that Greek culture survived and that religious apostasy was kept to a minimum.

Italian Rule and Union with Greece

The Ottomans brutally suppressed Rhodian attempts to join the 1821 Greek revolution on the mainland, and when an independent Greek state was finally established the island was not part of it. By the end of the 19th century the Ottoman Empire was in decline, but hopes of union with Greece were dashed in 1912 when Rhodes and the other Dodecanese fell to the Italians during a war with the Ottomans over Libya. Although a 1915 conference committed Italy to hand over the Dodecanese (except Rhodes) to Greece, the 1920 Treaty of Sèvres recognised Italian sovereignty.

After the Fascists came to power in 1922, they began a programme to make Rhodes more Italian. The entire townscape was replanned and many Mediterranean Art Deco and Rationalist structures erected. Though the Rhodians suffered considerable hardship under the occupation, the Italians made the island far more accessible with regular sea-plane services and built the first tourist hotels. They also excavated and restored ancient and medieval sites, and constructed roads and rural colonies.

Despite the Treaty of Sèvres being nullified by the 1923 Treaty of Lausanne, it became increasingly clear that Italy had no intention of ceding the

The Italians left their mark in Rhodes New Town

Dodecanese – or rather, the *Isole Italiane del'Egeo* – to Greece. In 1936, Italian became the official language, with both the Greek language and the Greek Orthodox Church suppressed.

Following Mussolini's capitulation in September 1943, German troops took over all Italian military bases in the Dodecanese. The islands were liberated one at a time by British forces between September 1944 and May 1945, and, after a 22-month occupation while the Italo-Greek peace treaty was finalised, they were handed over to the Greek military authorities on 31 March 1947. On 9 January 1948, the Dodecanese were officially annexed by Greece. Rhodes gained duty-free status, but mass tourism didn't really take off until the late 1960s. For most of that decade, Rhodes – especially Líndos – was largely a bohemian hangout. The first charters and package tours arrived in the early 1970s, which coincided with the construction of many hotels and apartments.

More recently, the island achieved some notoriety due to the misdemeanours of young revellers at Faliráki resort, which culminated in the fatal stabbing of a British youth in August 2003. The subsequent official crackdown was swift and severe, and Faliráki is now a shadow of its former self. In general, there has been a shift towards 'quality tourism', repositioning Rhodes as one of the most cosmopolitan destinations in the Mediterranean. The cobbled streets of the Old Town – designated a Unesco World Heritage site – are once again a Babel where many tongues can be heard, but these invaders are generally welcome.

Sun-worshippers congregate on Faliráki beach

Historical Landmarks

1450–1200BC Rhodes settled by Minoan Cretans, then Mycenaeans.

1150BC Invasion of the 'Sea Peoples'.

c.700BC Rhodian city-states found the Dorian Hexapolis.

408BC Ialysos, Lindos and Kameiros unite to establish Rhodes Town at the north tip of the island.

342BC School of rhetoric founded by Aeskhines.

305BC Unsuccessful siege of Rhodes by the Macedonian Demetrios Polyorketes; the Colossus is built afterwards.

227BC Colossus collapses in an earthquake which wrecks Rhodes.

42BC Cassius sacks the city and carries off many treasures to Rome.

AD58 St Paul visits Rhodes.

2nd–9th centuries AD The island is a Byzantine backwater, assailed by earthquakes, pirates and various invaders.

1309 Knights Hospitaller of St John assume control of Rhodes.

1440–80 Thanks to their strong fortifications, the Knights repel several attacks by the Egyptian and Ottoman sultans.

1523 The Knights surrender the island to Sultan Süleyman after a six-month siege, and retire to Malta.

16th century Ottoman mosques and baths built in the walled city; Orthodox *marásia* founded outside the walls.

1912 Italians oust Ottomans from Rhodes and the rest of the Dodecanese.

1923–39 First systematic archaeological excavations; Italian urban renewal and architectural monuments.

1940 Italy attacks Greece; Rhodes an important Italian base.

1943 Italy capitulates, Germans occupy Rhodes.

1944 Rhodian Jews deported; Rhodes Old Town sustains heavy damage in Allied bombardments.

1945 Germany surrenders Rhodes to the British.

1947 British hand over Dodecanese to Greek military governor.

1960s Beginning of mass tourism on Rhodes.

1988 Rhodes Old Town designated a Unesco World Heritage site.

2004 Establishment of Ecofilms documentary and features festival.

WHERE TO GO

Rhodes is an easy island to explore, with a good road network and public transport for those who want to sightsee independently. The old quarters of Rhodes Town and Líndos are mostly car-free, and are ideal places to wander through on foot. There are also numerous professional tour companies for those who want an organised itinerary.

This guide is divided into several sections, exploring Rhodes Old and New Town first. Then there's a tour of the eastern coast, with a separate section for the ancient settlement of Lindos and the area south of it, followed by another section covering the western side of the island.

RHODES OLD TOWN

Nothing quite prepares you for the spectacle of Rhodes **Old Town**. An immense citadel with high sandstone walls 4km (2½ miles) long, facing the town's three natural harbours, it immediately takes you back in time.

Built on the site of ancient Rhodes, itself founded some four centuries prior to the birth of Christ, the Old Town served from 1309 onwards as the headquarters of the Knights Hospitaller of St John, one of the most powerful of the Christian military Orders. Originally established to provide medical care for pilgrims on their journeys to the Holy Land, they soon became one of the leading military opponents of Islam, harrying both Arab and Kurdish armies and later the Ottoman Empire.

In December 1522, after a long siege, Ottoman forces wrested Rhodes from the grasp of the Knights and thus

The view along the east coast from Tsambíka Monastery

began nearly four centuries of Muslim Turkish rule. Vestiges of their influence are still obvious within the walls. The turn of the 20th century saw accelerated Ottoman decline and, in 1912, following the Italian-Turkish War, the Dodecanese islands (including Rhodes) were occupied by Italy. In contrast to the Ottoman neglect, the Italians invested considerable effort and money in the crown jewel of their new overseas colonies.

In the northernmost sector of the Old Town is the Knights' Quarter or Collachium (*kollákio* in Greek), where the *langues* had their inns and the Grand Master had his palace. Beyond this is the Boúrgo or civilian area, where you will find a fascinating maze of streets, comprising the former Turkish quarter and the old Jewish sector of the town.

The Walls and Gates

The first impressive feature of the town is the walls themselves. Dating mostly from preparations for the 1480 siege, they sit strong and proud, especially beautiful at dawn, rosy-hued in the sun's first rays, or at night, lit by the soft glow of wrought-iron lamps. The Knights did not begin the citadel from scratch; they elaborated a series of relatively modest Byzantine defences, creating eight sections of curtain walls, each one the responsibility of a separate *langue* or nationality that made up the Order of the Knights *(see page 36)*.

Conqueror's gate

Victorious Ottoman Sultan Süleyman entered the town through the southwesterly Ágios Athanásios Gate in 1523 and ordered it sealed up thereafter; it was only reopened by the Italians.

At one time each curtain had a gate; today there are 11 gates in use, each with its own design. Many are only wide enough to accept pedestrians or scooters. The most interesting is **Amboise Gate** – situated in the northwest corner near the Palace

Entering the Old Town through Amboise Gate

of the Grand Masters *(see page 35)*, it was built in 1512, during the reign of Grand Master Emery d'Amboise. It curves in an S-shape to outwit attackers and is then followed by a second gate, **Ágios Andónios** (St Anthony's), which lies between two inner curtain walls.

Near this gate is one of four discreetly signed entry tunnel-stairways leading to the **dry moat**, which has been attractively landscaped on the west and southeast sides. It is possible to follow a path in the moat from here all the way around the landward walls to the Akándia Gate on the east side of the city. The walk takes about 30 minutes. However, it is not possible to gain direct access to many of the gates on this route as they sit high in the walls above, with bridges over the moat linking the Old Town to the outside world.

On the eastern side of the fortifications, facing Kolóna Harbour, is the impressive Marine Gate *(see page 48)*, plus in the northeast, linking the Kolóna and Mandráki harbours, the smaller St Paul's Gate *(see page 47)*. In 1924 the Italians decided that traffic would need access along the waterfront. They altered the walls, creating widened entrances for automobiles on the shore between Mandráki and Kolóna ports. The most important of these, **Freedom Gate** (Pýli Eleftherías) is located just west of St Paul's Gate, isolating it and the Naillac Tower from the rest of the citadel. Today many visitors enter the Old Town through this gate as it is the nearest to the taxi stand and main bus stations.

The Knights' Quarter

All the living and administrative quarters of the Knights are at the northern end of the Old Town. Just inside the Freedom Gate lies **Platía Sými** (Sými Square), which holds the remnants of a 3rd-century BC **Temple of Aphrodite**. Only a few columns and a section of entablature are on view, though other remains were found in the ancient shipyards behind the two buildings to the west. One of these houses an **annexe** (Tue–Sat 8am–2pm and Fri 5–8pm; charge) of the Museum of Modern Greek Art *(see page 47)*, hosting temporary exhibitions.

Platía Argyrokástrou

Beyond the temple is **Platía Argyrokástrou**, decorated by a fountain with a dolphin spout. The base of the fountain is in fact a Byzantine baptismal font discovered by Italian archaeologists in the south of the island, but it doesn't look at all out of place here. The square is flanked on the east by the splendid **Inn of Auvergne**, built in the 16th century for the *langue* of Auvergne – one of three French-speaking *langues* within the Knights' Order *(see page 36)*.

Behind the fountain is a building of 14th-century origin thought to have been the original hospital for the Order, although it was later used as an arsenal – Oplothíki in Greek, its modern official name. It now houses the archives of the Dodecanesian Institute of Archaeology, as well as (in the south wing) the **Decorative Arts Museum**. This comprises an interesting collection of embroidery, pottery, traditional costumes and woodcarvings – the best of the latter being carved cupboard doors and chest lids. One section displays an entire Rhodian single-room house complete with household tools and accessories.

Platía Argyrokástrou

Museum Square

Further south, through the archway, is **Platía Mousíou** (Museum Square), flanked by several important buildings. On the eastern side is the church of **Panagía tou Kástrou** (Our Lady of the Castle), built by the Byzantines and completed by the Knights, who made it into their cathedral. Its austere stone walls retain faint 14th-century fresco fragments from its time as a Christian place of worship, though it became a mosque during the Ottoman period. Today, the church is home to the **Byzantine Museum** (Tue–Sun 8.30am–2.40pm; charge), displaying a collection of powerful icons, mostly from the 14th and 15th centuries, and post-Byzantine frescoes rescued from neglected churches on Rhodes and the surrounding islands.

At the southeastern corner of the square, by the **Arnáldou Gate**, stands the **Inn of England** (1483), rebuilt by the Italians after it was destroyed in 1856.

The courtyard of the Archaeological Museum

Archaeological Museum

The western side of Museum Square is dominated by one of the most important buildings in the Old Town – the Knights' New Hospital, which now houses the **Archaeological Museum of Rhodes** (summer Tue–Sun 8am–7.10pm, winter Tue–Sun 8.30am–2.40pm; charge). As well as displaying finds from all the ancient sites on the island, the building itself pays testament to the wealth of the Order and the considerable engineering prowess of its medieval builders.

Construction began in 1440 under Grand Master Jean Bonpart de Lastic, after the previous Grand Master, Antoine de Fluvian, bequeathed a 10,000 gold florin building fund, but the building was not fully completed until 1489 under Grand Master Pierre d'Aubusson. The hospital was state-of-the-art for its time, and its doctors treated Christians from all over Europe. Restoration began during the Italian era, with more needed following bomb damage in World War II.

Inside the building is a large **courtyard** flanked by arched porticoes, one of them graced by a lion statue of Hellenistic origin. There are also piles of cannonballs used in various sieges against the town, including those of Süleyman the Magnificent.

To the left of the courtyard, a stone staircase leads up to the **infirmary room**. A vast open space, with a roof supported by several stone columns, it gives the impression of a medieval courtroom. This was the main ward of the hospital, with a capacity for over 100 beds and several small recessed rooms for the very sick. It had a fireplace at one end but very few other luxuries. Today, the room houses relics from the era of the Knights. The gravestones of illustrious members are on display here, with coats-of-arms depicting several lineages.

The rooms on the rest of the floor, including the large refectory, have been divided into smaller spaces to display mostly painted pottery, *pithoi* (urns) and grave artefacts found at ancient Ialysos and Kameiros, as well as other sites on the island. Rooms 6 to 8 display finds from Ialysos, which range from the 9th to the 4th century BC, while rooms 9 to 15 display finds from Kameiros. Both sites were initially excavated during the Italian period.

The **atrium** area to the north, which was once the hospital kitchen, contains some splendid Classical statuary and grave steles, in particular one donated by Krito for her mother Timarista. It was carved around 410BC by a local artist, in the Athenian style prevalent at the time, and was found at Kameiros. Nearby is an Archaic-era *kouros* and a small head of

Portrait bust of Helios

Zeus found near his temple on Mount Atávyros.

Other rooms display very fine Hellenistic and Roman statuary, including two marble versions of Aphrodite: *Thalassia* or *Aidoumene*, celebrated by Lawrence Durrell as the 'Marine Venus' but lent a rather eerie aspect by her sea-dissolved face, and the more accessible *Aphrodite Bathing*, with the goddess crouched and fanning out her hair. This was carved in the 1st century BC

The beautiful *Aphrodite Bathing*

but is considered to be a copy of a 3rd-century BC work. On the same level is a sculpture garden with a curious collection of stylised beasts real and mythical – a dolphin head, a lion and a sea serpent – posed among potted plants.

Street of the Knights

North of the museum is **Odós Ippotón** (Street of the Knights), where many of the Inns of the Order were based. One of the most complete medieval streets in the world, its buildings are of finely chiselled sandstone forming one uninterrupted facade that rises to a double archway spanning the road at its peak. Small square windows and fine arched doorways pierce the masonry – doors wide enough for horse and carriage or a single rider atop his steed. There are many other small details to be seen here, including carved masonry and commemorative plaques.

During the day Odós Ippotón is crowded with strolling visitors and large tour groups striding to the next location on their itinerary. This can make it difficult to imagine Knights arriving on horseback or walking between inns for strategy meetings, or the lower-ranking brothers heading to the hospital for their medical duties. It is easier to imagine yourself back in the 14th century at night, when the street takes on a more magical atmosphere with the waxy glow of the streetlights reminiscent of medieval oil-lamps, and the only sound is the gurgle of the fountain in the Villaragut Mansion garden.

The first building on the right (north) is the **Inn of Italy**, with a plaque honouring Grand Master Fabrizio del Carretto (1513–21) above its entranceway. Next to it is the smaller **Palace of Philippe Villiers de l'Isle-Adam**, the immediate successor of Carretto, and the Grand Master ousted by Süleyman in 1522.

Across the street, further uphill you will see a small garden with a trickling Ottoman fountain surrounded by cannon-

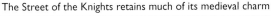

The Street of the Knights retains much of its medieval charm

balls; this is the courtyard of the 15th-century **Villaragut Mansion**, restored in 2002 but seldom open to the public. Immediately across the street stands the highly decorated **Inn of France**, where a splendid life-sized carving of a knight in repose is set in stone – perhaps once a tombstone – just inside the courtyard, which also has a chapel dating from the era of Grand Master Raymond Beranger (1365–74), though the street frontage dates from over a century later.

Near the top of Ippotón are two final inns, those of **Provence** (1418), on the right, and **Spain**, on the left, which housed two separate *langues*, those of Aragón and Castile. Around 1462, Grand Master Pedro Raymondo Zacosta contrived to divide the Spanish *langue* into that of Aragón (actually Catalan-speaking) and Castile, in a move to counter the overwhelming influence of the French inns.

At the very top of the street, to the left, are the remains of the **Church of St John of the Collachium**, named after the Order's patron, where the Grand Masters were buried. The Ottomans used its basement as a gunpowder magazine, and in 1856 lightning set off a powerful explosion that not only vaporised the church, but destroyed much of the town and killed over 800 people.

Restoring the Street of the Knights

Grand Tourists and Belle Époque travellers noted the picturesque dilapidation of the Street of the Knights, where Muslim families had adapted the grand inns for their needs by adding projected wooden structures with latticed gratings to upper-floor windows. These served to protect the virtue of the womenfolk from prying eyes, while allowing them in turn to survey the street. When the Italians took control of the island, these additions were summarily swept away and restoration carried out according to notions of a vanished medieval ideal.

Many mosaics in the Palace of the Grand Masters are from Kos

Palace of the Grand Masters

At the top of the Street of the Knights is the **Palace of the Grand Masters**. This was the administrative heart and power base of the Order of the Knights of St John and the most important building in the Knights' Quarter. Left to fall into a state of disrepair by the Ottomans – they used it as a prison before the 1856 explosion nearly levelled it – it was renovated by the Italians with results that remain controversial for a number of reasons. The original ground-plan of the palace was not adhered to, with many modernising features added to the interior – including statuary and mosaics brought from other Dodecanese islands, which still resent the loss of these treasures.

Greek archaeologists would have preferred to demolish the ruins of the palace to excavate the site in search of a Classical temple thought to lie directly beneath. However, the Italians saw an opportunity to create an impressive summer palace for their royal family (none of whom ever used it), and so the palace was rebuilt. However, the Italians employed poor-quality materials and workmanship, even by the standards of the 1930s, which has resulted in frequent, costly repairs since the 1990s as the reinforced concrete core of the building corrodes and expands.

The Order of the Knights

The Order had three classes of membership, each bound by vows of chastity, poverty and obedience. Fully fledged Knights were recruited from Europe's noblest families and numbered around 650, commoners could serve as soldiers or nurses, while chaplains saw to their spiritual needs. There were eight *langues* or 'tongues': English, German, French, Provençal, Auvergnat, Aragonese (in fact Catalan), Castilian and Italian. Each *langue* lived in a compound called an inn, under an appointed prior. For security, they went about in pairs and left the walled domain only on horseback.

French influence outweighed the other tongues when it came to electing the lifelong post of Grand Master. Thus, 14 of the 19 Grand Masters were from one of the French *langues*, and French was the Order's spoken language (Latin for official documents). The Italians' maritime talents made them the obvious choice to command the fleet, while other tongues each defended a section, or 'curtain', of the city walls.

After being expelled from Rhodes, the knights were without a base for seven years, until the island of Malta was offered to them by Holy Roman Emperor Charles V. They changed their name to the Knights of Malta and successfully repelled a four-month Ottoman siege in 1565. Despite this, the Order was fast becoming obsolete; nations could now outfit their own fleets more efficiently, and the new trade routes to the Americas and the Far East dwarfed the significance of the Mediterranean.

Nowadays the Order has been revived in many countries (including England's St John Ambulance Brigade) and engages in many medical and charitable activities. You can learn more at www.orderofmalta.org.

Despite these issues, the building rarely fails to impress, retaining a majesty that befits its old role. Columns and capitals from ancient sites have been used throughout the interior, and the exterior stone cladding shows how the whole of the Knights' Quarter would have appeared in its prime. Look for the magnificent wooden ceilings, and the translucent panes of onyx in the windows that let in a soft light. Many of the main rooms have spectacular

Palace battlements

Hellenistic and Roman mosaics taken from sites across nearby Kos, and although it is ethically questionable whether they should be here, they have been carefully preserved.

The palace's entrance is between two imposing semicircular towers; a grand marble staircase leads to the upper-floor rooms, airy though sparsely furnished to allow a better appreciation of the structure and mosaics. The latter include depictions of the Nine Muses, another with a nymph on a sea-horse, and another showing the head of Medusa; fish and dolphins are also popular themes.

The ground-floor rooms, which originally acted as stables or grain and munitions stores during the great sieges, flank a courtyard sporting a series of Classical statues. These rooms house a permanent exhibition of finds from the first 2,400 years of Rhodes' history, as well as a medieval gallery covering the period up to the Ottoman conquest, plus there are temporary exhibitions. The collections are excellent – better organised and labelled than the Archaeological Museum.

Odós Sokrátous is lined with shops, cafés and restaurants

The Boúrgo

At the time of the Knights, the rest of the town's civilian population, though not permitted to live within the Collachium, still resided within the city walls. After the Ottoman conquest, only Muslims and Jews were allowed to live in the citadel, and the town acquired a new profile as mosques were built and minarets pierced the skyline. Although some Ottoman buildings were destroyed after their departure, most survive (though often in poor condition), and one of the mosques is still in use.

Odós Sokrátous and Platía Ippokrátous

The area still has many fascinating corners to explore. A maze of pebble-paved alleyways – some busy with people, others deserted – leads to hidden corners where you never know what's around the next bend, yet no matter where you wander, you won't get hopelessly lost – everything eventually leads back to a main thoroughfare, **Odós Sokrátous**

(Socrates Street), where there are plenty of shops, cafés and restaurants. This has been the main commercial thorough-fare since ancient times, though the Ottomans with their flair for bazaar culture accentuated its role.

Early in the morning before the shopfronts have opened, Sokrátous appears much as it did a century or so ago. Later in the day, however, tour and cruise-ship patrons crowd the pavements, and the windows of the numerous shops along the main drag and in the little alleyways either side display everything from gold jewellery and designer watches to fake handbags and tacky postcards. The patter of the merchants offering 'bargains' is good-natured but persistent, so few visitors leave empty-handed.

At the western end of the street, where it meets Odós Orféos and Odós Ippodámou, are several important build-ings. The most impressive is **Süleymaniye Mosque**, with its magenta-tinted walls and distinctive minaret. This mosque, built in 1523 to mark the Ottoman takeover of the island, has emerged from a long renovation process (including a new minaret), but is still not yet officially open to the public and so can only be viewed from the outside. A small flight of steps on Odós Orféos affords the best views of the large dome that tops the building.

Süleymaniye Mosque

Odós Orféos also leads to the **Rolói** (open all day and evening; charge), a clock tower erected in 1851 on the site of a Byzantine-era tower. The tower gives impressive views over the Old Town's rooftops; you can clearly see what a labyrinth it is and yet how small an area it covers.

The Kastellanía on Platía Ippokrátous dates from 1507

Opposite the mosque at the intersection of Sokrátous and Odós Ippodámou is a **Muslim library**, founded in 1794; among its priceless collection of Persian and Arabic manuscripts are a number of rare handwritten Korans dating from the 15th and 16th centuries. The elegant Arabic script around the doorway will tell you that you are in the right place.

The other building, right at the corner, is the **Imaret** (the *Palió Syssítio* in Greek), once an almshouse for theological students; today it houses a very pleasant café in its lovely vaulted interior (plus tables outside), and a gallery (Tue–Sat 10am–2pm) across the pebble-paved courtyard hosting periodic art exhibits.

The east end of Sokrátous opens out onto **Platía Ippokrátous** (Hippocrates Square), one of the main meeting places in the Old Town, a few steps south of the Marine Gate with its massive towers. In the centre of the square is the **Syndriváni**, a fountain topped by an Italian ornament and normally bedecked by pigeons. In the southeastern corner of the square, the stone building called the **Kastellanía** was the medieval courthouse and commercial tribunal of the Knights, completed in 1507 and restored by the Italians between 1925 and 1935. The building now houses the public library and town archives.

The Turkish Quarter

South of Sokrátous lies the heart of the former **Turkish Quarter**, perhaps the most intriguing area in the Old Town. Narrow twisting lanes lead to empty squares, disused, semi-derelict mosques, Neoclassical mansion facades, Ottoman

The Turks of Rhodes

The Turkish community of Rhodes was established in 1523, when an Ottoman garrison and civil servants settled principally in and around the main town. Their numbers were boosted between 1898 and 1913 by Greek-speaking Muslims fleeing unsettled conditions on Crete. These refugees founded the seaside suburb of Kritiká, about 3km (2 miles) southwest.

Some Old Town Turks claim to trace their ancestry to the original conquest, and feel that they have every right to be considered native Rhodians. However, the Greek authorities rarely agree, and their bureaucratic treatment of the Rhodian Turks often reflects the current state of relations between Greece and Turkey. The years after 1948 saw a sharp decline in the Muslim population, from about 6,500 to under 2,000. Around 1974, when the war in Cyprus made the position of Rhodian Turks very precarious, many wealthier Muslims sold their property in Rhodes Old Town and Líndos at knockdown prices.

However, since a European Court of Human Rights decision in 1997, Rhodian Turks cannot be stripped of Greek nationality no matter how long they have been resident in Turkey, Australia or elsewhere, and can return freely. As a result the local population has stabilised at around 2,500.

wooden balconies and ochre or powder-blue stucco-rendered ancient walls. The beautiful stone buttresses arching overhead are designed to provide structural support in the event of an earthquake. In the evenings, as taverna street-tables begin to fill, this area awakens from its mid-afternoon sleep.

Streets such as **Agíou Fanouríou**, **Pythagóra** and **Sofokléous** make good starting points for exploration, and if you begin to feel jaded try a Turkish bath (Mon–Fri 10am–6pm, Sat 8am–6pm, Sun 10am–3pm; charge) at the renovated **Mustafa Hamam** on Platía Aríonos, next to the minaret-less **Mustafa Mosque**, now used as an events hall.

The Jews of Rhodes

Jews have lived on Rhodes since the 2nd century BC. In return for their support during the 1522 siege, the Ottomans assigned the Jews their own quarter in the east of the walled city. Under the Italians, who favoured them as a counter to Greek nationalism, the Jewish population reached a high of around 4,000 by the 1920s.

Thereafter, the Rodesli (as Rhodian Jews call themselves) began to emigrate in large numbers to the Belgian Congo, Rhodesia, Egypt, South America and the US. By the time anti-Semitic laws were promulgated and enforced in 1938–9, and war broke out between Italy and the Allies shortly after, some 2,000 Rodesli were safely overseas, avoiding the fate of the 1,973 Rodesli and 120 Jews from Kos deported to Auschwitz by the Nazis in July 1944.

Of these, just 161 (plus 53 with Turkish nationality, who were saved by Turkey's consul in Rhodes) survived. Today there are under 40 in Rhodes Town, mostly elderly Jews from the Greek mainland, who resettled here early in the 1960s on the orders of Greece's head rabbi to ensure a continued Jewish presence on the island. The last community-supported rabbi left Rhodes in 1936, so one comes annually from Israel to conduct Yom Kippur services.

The Jewish Quarter

From Platía Ippokrátous at the eastern end of Odós Sokrátous, Odós Aristotélous extends east towards **Platía Evréon Martýron** (Square of the Jewish Martyrs), which is named in honour of the inhabitants of the adjacent Jewish Quarter who were sent to Auschwitz by the Nazis in the summer of 1944. At the centre of the square is a black granite memorial to the victims. Flanking the *platía* on its north is the 15th-century **Navarhío** or Admiralty of the Knights; this later became the seat of the local Orthodox Archbishop.

A quiet back street

The **Kal Kadosh Shalom Synagogue** (Apr–Oct Sun–Fri 10am–3pm; donation; www.rhodesjewishmuseum.org), on Odós Simíou, just off the square, was first built in the 16th century and has been carefully renovated with funds sent by emigrated Jewish Rhodians; to one side is an excellent three-room **museum** which thematically covers the community's history both in Rhodes Town and overseas.

Heading east out of the square towards the Pýli Panagías (Virgin's Gate) opening onto Kolóna Harbour, you'll pass the ruined **Panagía tou Boúrgou** church, which was almost completely destroyed by bombing in World War II. Only the Gothic three-tiered apse remains standing; a little stage within sometimes hosts special events.

Ágios Nikólaos Fort sits in Mandráki Harbour

RHODES NEW TOWN

During the Turkish occupation, the Greek population and others who were not allowed to live in the Old Town inhabited the area immediately outside the city walls. Once distinct villages with their own parish churches, over time these settlements have grown together to form Rhodes **New Town**.

Mandráki Harbour

Just north of Freedom Gate, **Mandráki Harbour**, once the main port for the ancient city, is a favourite spot for Rhodians to take their regular *vólta* (evening stroll). The long easterly quay with its three **windmills** has anchorage for numerous private sailboats from around Europe. At the far end of this jetty sits **Ágios Nikólaos Fort**, originally built by the Knights and last used militarily during World War II. Today it supports a lighthouse to assist the modern vessels that negotiate these busy shallows. At the north end of the quay, the harbour's distinctive entrance comes into view. Despite wishful thinking and its portrayal on tea-towels, T-shirts and posters, the ancient Colossus never actually stood here. Today, two columns frame the opening, topped by two bronze **statues** of a doe and stag.

During summer, the southwest quays are home to numerous hydrofoils, catamarans and colourful excursion boats, which head down the coast to Líndos, or across to nearby islands. Immediately across the busy boulevard from this quay stands the orientalised Art Deco **Néa Agorá** (New Market), built by the Italians on the site of a much older bazaar. This serves as a focus of transport activity, with a main taxi rank and the bus station just outside. The interior is largely disappointing in terms of shops and tavernas, but at the centre is a wonderful raised open rotunda, originally a fish market.

Further along the west quay is the Italian-built cathedral of St John, today the Orthodox **Cathedral of Evangelismós** (Annunciation). It is worth trying to gain admission (easiest on Sunday) to see the frescoes painted between 1951–61 by Fotis Kontoglou, the great neo-Byzantine artist from Asia Minor – especially the *Annunciation* on the north wall, the *Virgin Platytéra* in the conch of the apse, and the *Psalmody* on the south wall, with figures holding period instruments.

The three famous windmills

Around the church is the **Foro Italico**, the main administrative buildings built by the Italians. When the Italians took control of the island, they set about redeveloping the northern part of the New Town, now known as **Neohóri**, giving it a new street plan and building the whimsical Governor's Palace, Town Hall, Courthouse, Port Authority (once the Fascist HQ), Post Office and the severe Municipal Theatre. These buildings were erected in two phases (1924–7 and 1932–9) by distinguished architects working first in orientalised Art Deco, and later the more severe Rationalist (essentially updated Neoclassical) styles, impelled by the social imperatives of Fascism. Since the millennium these buildings have received some long-overdue recognition and conservation work.

Just north of the theatre looms the bulbous-topped minaret of the **Murad Reis Mosque**, which was renovated in 2008. Peer through the wrought-iron railings at the exquisitely carved if neglected headstones of the old cemetery, one of the few that the Italians left alone during their remodelling. Murad Reis, one of Süleyman's admirals, met his end during the 1522 siege, and is buried in the circular mausoleum beside the mosque.

Élli Beach

Beyond the mosque is **Élli**, the main town beach, backed at the east end by the domed, Italian-built bathing establishment (home to a seasonally changing nightclub) and at the centre by the enormous casino, the largest in Greece, originally the Italian Albergo delle Rose, which still has a few rooms for high-rollers. At the western end of the beach and on the very northern tip of the island stands the Italian-built **Aquarium** (Enydrío; daily

Élli beach, with the Aquarium in the background

Apr–Sept 9am–8.30pm, Oct–Mar 9am–4.30pm; charge), with subterranean tanks full of creatures that live in the seas around Rhodes, plus interesting displays about the building itself.

Immediately south of here, on the oval plaza popularly known as Ekatón Hourmadiés (100 Date-Palms), is the **Museum of Modern Greek Art** (Tue–Sat 8am–2pm, Fri 8am–2pm and 5–8pm; charge), the richest collection of 20th-century Greek painting outside of Athens: all the big names – semi-abstract Níkos Hatzikyriákos-Ghíkas, Spýros Vassilíou, Yiánnis Tsaroúhis with his trademark portraits of young men, surrealist Níkos Engonópoulos, naïve artist Theóphilos, neo-Byzantinist Fótis Kóntoglou – are well represented.

Kolóna Harbour

Southeast of Mandráki Harbour you can walk along the waterside and through **St Paul's Gate**, an outer defensive bastion of the Old Town, emerging at the northwest end of

Fishing boats in Kolóna Harbour

Kolóna, the commercial harbour, busy with the movements of colourful fishing boats, commercial ferries, cruise ships and large catamarans. A favourite vantage point is the remains of the **Naillac Tower** just east of St Paul's Gate, with unrivalled views towards Mandráki, particularly at dawn and dusk. Just south of Kolóna's fishing port stands one of the most dramatic entrances to the walled town, the **Marine Gate**, flanked by two large round towers and retaining remnants of the mechanisms that operated the gate in past ages.

South and West New Town

Most of the modern town extends south and west of the Old Town. Just 2km (just over 1 mile, less than half an hour's walk) west of the citadel, the high ground of **Monte Smith** (Ágios Stéfanos). Signposts often say 'Akrópoli', as the Italian renaming of the heights after Sir Sydney Smith, a 19th-century British admiral who established a lookout point here during the Napoleonic Wars, is now falling into disfavour. At 110m (365ft) high, the summit offers an excellent view of the whole town, the surrounding islands and the Turkish coast, particularly at sunset. The hill is also home to the ruined Doric **Temple of Apollo** (always open), of which three columns and an architrave were re-erected by the Italians.

The distance from here to Kolóna gives you a good idea of the ancient city's size – nearly as extensive as modern Rhodes. Below the temple are the scant remains of an ancient *odeion* (theatre) and a stadium.

Rodíni Park (daily dawn to dusk; free), 3km (2 miles) south of the Ágios Athanásios Gate, is the place to go to cool off on a hot day. Fragrant conifers shade this parkland where the Knights used to cultivate medicinal herbs, while shrieking peacocks patrol either side of an Ottoman aqueduct. Walking trails loop around and across a spring-fed stream, interrupted by little dams to the delight of the resident ducks. Scholars say that this was the location of the famous ancient school of oratory; nowadays every August there's a nocturnal festival with grilled *souvláki* and all the Rhodian wine you can drink for a set price. At other times a recently refurbished bar-restaurant operates near the main entrance.

Oh Deer

Prompted by the Delphic Oracle, small fallow deer *(Dama dama)* – about the size of a greyhound – were introduced to Rhodes during ancient times to combat the island's snakes. These were said to be repelled by the odour of the deer's urine, or dispatched using their sharp antlers (though accounts vary). The Knights apparently introduced more as game, but during Ottoman times they were hunted exhaustively, and the Italians had to restock them.

For some years after the union of Rhodes with Greece, many semi-tame deer lived in the Old Town's moat, but after eight were killed by feral dogs in 1994, plans were made to safeguard the survivors. Some deer have been released into the wild interior and south of the island – where they are occasionally hit by cars – while dozens of others live more safely in a large, green-fenced reserve on the clifftop flanking the canyon in Rodíni Park.

The Mikrí Rotónda overlooks the coast at Pigés Kallithéas

THE NORTHEAST COAST

Rhodes' eastern coast is sheltered from the prevailing summer winds blowing down from the Aegean. The shoreline presents a mix of wide sandy bays and small pebbly coves, with sculpted limestone bluffs interrupting the flow of the main coastal road. In addition to several seaside resorts, there are numerous interesting excursions into the hills.

Kallithéa and Faliráki

Travelling south from Rhodes, the first resort is **Kallithéa**, which is soon followed by the mock-Moorish, Art Deco spa of **Pigés Kallithéas** (daily 8am–8pm; charge), 7km (4½ miles) from Rhodes. Healing springs have flowed here since ancient times, and the Ottomans maintained a bathing establishment here from the 1880s onwards. The current Italian-built spa dates from 1929 and has recently emerged from a lengthy restoration. The iconic image of the place is the dome of the **Mikrí Rotónda** in its clump of palms, just inland from a swimming lido used by scuba classes and a fancy bar serving from inside the original artificial grottoes.

The sprawling **Megáli Rotónda** higher up hosts changing modern art exhibitions and a permanent collection of still photos showing the spa in its post-war heyday and as it was when it featured in 1961's *The Guns of Navarone*. Though the waters no longer flow, the bigger rotonda is also regularly hired out as a venue for banquets and photo shoots.

From Pigés Kallithéas, the coast road continues towards the first hotels on **Faliráki Bay**, one of the best beaches on the island and unsurprisingly exploited for tourism. Towards the south end of the sand is **Faliráki** town, long notorious as one of the Mediterranean's top nightlife meccas. However, following a drink-fuelled crime spree in 2003 (including one murder), local police clamped down hard and the party moved on to Zákynthos in the Ionians.

Faliráki is now struggling to reinvent itself as a resort for families and young couples. Just a handful of the bars and mega-clubs survive from the dozens here at the resort's zenith. By day the beach remains busy as it is the parasailing hotspot of the Dodecanese. There are also ringos and banana rides on offer, as well as hundreds of umbrellas for the more sedentary to lie under. Near the south end of the strip is the original village's fishing anchorage and chapel, with a couple of tavernas that serve traditional Greek fare situated nearby.

Perfect Koskinoú

Inland from Kallithéa, the village of Koskinoú is noted for its clusters of traditional 18th-century Rhodian houses, which are kept in pristine condition. Every door and window frame receives a regular dose of bright paint, and the whole effect is enhanced with plants in ceramic pots.

Afándou and Eptá Pigés

Afándou, 5km (3 miles) south of Faliráki, is the next major settlement, situated inland from the centre of a long, eponymous bay. Just as you enter the coastal plain, there are signposts to the only 18-hole golf course on Rhodes. The island's climate means that greens here often have a decidedly brown appearance, and the fairways are said to be extra firm. Afándou means 'invisible', referring to the fact that the village cannot be seen from the sea, which protected it from medieval pirate raids. The village's inhabitants have cultivated orchards of stone fruits such as apricots for many generations, and the local carpet-weaving tradition only recently died out. The beach itself, minimally developed other than sun longers and showers, is one of Rhodes' best. The most scenic portion is Traganoú at the north end, where there are rock formations and caves to explore.

Anthony Quinn Bay

Tucked into the headland of Ladikó closing off Faliráki Bay to the south is scenic, rock-girt 'Anthony Quinn Bay', named in honour of the actor, who fell in love with Rhodes while here filming *The Guns of Navarone*.

From Afándou it is possible to travel via the village of Psínthos to Petaloúdes (Valley of the Butterflies), which is described on *pages 65–6*.

From the crossroads at Kolýmbia further south, a road leads inland to **Eptá Pigés** (Seven Springs), the perfect antidote to hot summer days in town or on the beach. This oasis has been exploited by farmers since

Ottoman times; later, the Italians planted a pine forest to shelter numerous species of wild orchids, and their engineers channelled the springs to form a small artificial lake in the forest.

Many visitors enjoy following the route of the springs from their origin, paddling through above-ground channels into a large tunnel that passes under a nearby hillside to the reservoir. You can traverse the tunnel, nearly 200m (650ft) long, with the aid of a torch, but watch out for people coming back in the other direction – it's not really made for two-way traffic. For the claustrophobic, there is also an over-

Following the route of the spring water at Eptá Pigés

ground tunnel that makes the trip to the same spot. Alternatively, visitors can sit in the shady café and watch the ducks, geese and peacocks strut about.

Tsambíka

Tsambíka Monastery sits on the peak of a rocky promontory overlooking the coast just a little further south of Eptá Pigés. Although a narrow, steep concrete lane leads most of the way there, female pilgrims usually walk (or crawl on hands and knees) from the main road to pray for fertility and the chance of a child, especially during the festival on 8 September. Though modern fertility treatments have lowered

A pretty bloom

their numbers, you will still find many children called Tsambíka or Tsambíkos – a sure sign that the Virgin answered their mother's prayer. Even from the parking lot there are still 298 steps up to the pinnacle, a breathtaking walk in all senses of the word. Once there, the tiny modern church itself is disappointing, but the views are definitely not.

Some 326m (1,060ft) directly below is sandy **Tsambíka Bay**, which has many watersports franchises but only one permanent building. Gently shelving, it is the first beach on the islands that becomes swimmable in April. Beyond this, several bays are visible as far as Líndos, and other rugged limestone promontories fill the panorama.

Arhángelos to Líndos

Further south, **Arhángelos**, guarded by its Knights' castle, is one of the largest villages on the island. It has remained outside the tourist mainstream, making a living largely from farming. There are still a few ceramic kilns and showrooms, especially on the main bypass road, but only one traditional boot-maker remains of the several which once supplied the high-cut, supple footwear designed to guard against both snakes and thornbushes. From Arhángelos a twisty, steep road leads down to the small beach resort at **Stegná**, which has an excellent taverna and is not overdeveloped.

Further along the main road, a left turn leads to **Haráki**, where several tavernas lining the seafront. Above the village is **Feraklós Castle**, once one of the largest fortifications on the island. Unfortunately, little remains of the castle today, but in its prime it must have been impressive – it was the first position established by the Knights in 1306, and the last to surrender to Ottoman forces in the 1520s, well after Rhodes Town itself had fallen. The road that leads to the castle continues on to the gently shelving **Agía Agathí** beach just north. Perhaps the sandiest on Rhodes, it is a popular destination for excursion boats, with plenty of watersports on offer and several beach bars.

The main east-coast highway crosses the wide **Mássari Plain** on its way south. Hidden among the area's main citrus orchards is an old airstrip used by both the Italian and German forces during World War II. Eventually, after passing the turnoff for superb, unspoilt **Kálathos** beach, the road rounds a rocky outcrop and reveals a photogenic view of the citadel and village of Líndos.

The village of Arhángelos retains a traditional feel

Líndos village sits beneath the ancient Acropolis

LÍNDOS AND THE SOUTHEAST

In ancient times **Lindos** was the most cosmopolitan and commercial of Rhodes' three original city-states. Its 'golden age' occurred during the 6th century BC under the tyrant Kleoboulos, considered one of the 'seven sages' of the ancient world – in ancient times the title 'tyrant' did not have the pejorative associations of today. It was he who established the Temple of Athena on the Acropolis, which allowed Lindos to retain its status as the island's most important religious sanctuary even after Rhodes Town was founded in 408BC.

Perched upon a sheer-sided coastal precipice, this site was always an excellent stronghold, and the Byzantines and Knights both fortified the site before it fell into decline during Ottoman rule. The village of Líndos remained a historical backwater, aside from a brief period of prosperity in late medieval times, when its sea captains plied the entire Mediterranean and built themselves sumptuous houses. Eventually in the 1960s bohemian types favoured the village as an idyllic hangout and the fashionable set soon followed; money rolled in to renovate the captains' mansions and create a whitewashed 'postcard-perfect' settlement.

Líndos Village

Today Líndos has a permanent population of just a few hundred people – most Lindians now live in nearby villages and commute here to work in the all-dominating tourist trade. As one of the most photographed locations in the Aegean, the village can get unbearably crowded in high season. If you wish to wander in peace and sense some of the atmosphere of the place it is advisable to come early or outside peak season. Most vehicles are banned from the village itself, with parking allowed only on the outskirts. Buses and taxis drop visitors in the Indian-fig-shaded square with its gurgling fountain. From here a maze of narrow streets criss-cross the lower hill, the main ones lined with souvenir shops, noisy bars and restaurants with roof gardens that provide an excellent bird's-eye view.

Líndos is one place on Rhodes where you can still find the traditional *monóhoro* or one-room house – given by a girl's family as a dowry on her marriage. Surrounded by high walls with ornate gateways, these dwellings,

Kleoboulos' tomb

Such pithy maxims as 'nothing in excess', inscribed at the sanctuary at Delphi on the mainland, are ascribed to the Lindian ruler Kleoboulos. A round Hellenistic structure on the headland of Ágios Emilianós – now a chapel – is purported to be the great sage's tomb, but since it was built five centuries too late it seems unlikely to be his actual resting place.

Kímisis Theotókou church

usually divided inside by a soaring arch, had outer court-yards whose floors were laid with a mosaic of pebbles or *votsalotó*, and flanked the kitchen and other extra rooms that were built subsequently. Today, many are holiday studios managed by package tour operators. The grander captains' mansions are usually expatriate properties, or have been converted into restaurants or bars. One that isn't, the **Papakonstandís Mansion**, functions as a museum.

The route to the Acropolis, which is indicated by small hand-painted signs, passes the tall stone campanile and red-tile roof of the **Kímisis Theotókou** church (Dormition of the Mother of God; Mon–Sat 9am–3pm and 4.30–6pm, Sun 9am–3pm). It contains exquisite post-Byzantine frescoes by Gregory of Sými, as well as a fine *votsalotó* floor.

The Acropolis

The climb to the **Acropolis** (Tue–Sun 8am–6.45pm, Mon 12.30–6.45pm; charge) is steep, made more arduous in summer by the dry, hot air that hangs heavily in the often wind-less village. An alternative is to ride a donkey to the top – the station is by the main square – for about five euros. These are just about the only working donkeys left on Rhodes, as most have been replaced by modern farming machinery. The route towards the looming walls passes women peddling lace and cotton fabric and affords inviting views over the invitingly azure sea with excursion caiques and expensive speedboats moored offshore.

A ticket booth sits inside the citadel's lower gate, just before a monumental staircase to the summit. At the bottom of the steps on the rocks to the left there is a **relief of a Hellenistic trireme** (warship). At the top is the **Residence of the Knights' Commander**, which adjoins the remains of the Byzantine **Ágios Ioánnis** (St John).

Beyond the church is the base of the main ancient site, the **Sanctuary of Athena Lindia**. The sanctuary is entered via a large **Hellenistic stoa** (covered walkway), 87m (285ft) long and constructed around 200BC, which would have contained shops selling offerings to take into the sanctuary. Beyond the stoa, a wide staircase leads to the **propylaia** – the entrance to the sanctuary itself. This consisted of a series of colonnades surrounding the inner **Temple of Athena Lindia** at the highest seaward point on the rock. The remains seen today – several columns of the propylaia and inner *bemas* (raised

There are fantastic views from the ancient Acropolis

platforms) – date from 342BC; the original sanctuary built by Kleoboulos was destroyed by fire in 392BC.

The Knights' 14th-century fortifications offer superb views of **Líndos Bay** to the north, the town to the west, and perfectly sheltered **St Paul's Bay** to the south. This was where St Paul supposedly landed when thrown off course by a fierce storm in AD58. The gap in the rocks here is said to have been miraculously opened by lightning, allowing his boat to land safely. A small, whitewashed church marks the spot.

Inland to Láerma

Beyond Líndos, the coast road passes through **Péfki** resort, with its secluded coves at the base of low cliffs, and **Lárdos** village slightly inland, also well geared to tourism. From Lárdos it's 12km (7 miles) to **Láerma** village, which, like many in this part of the island, has lost its younger population to the coastal resorts and Rhodes Town, leaving the older folks to tend crops or chat over coffee at the *kafenío*.

Begun in the 9th century, **Thárri Monastery**, 5km (3 miles) south of Láerma, is the oldest on Rhodes. Now home to a small community of monks, its church (open during daylight hours) shelters stunning, well-cleaned frescoes dating from 1300 to 1450.

South to Prassonísi

South of Péfki, the next major coastal resort is **Kiotári**, which sprung up in the mid-1990s with several luxury hotels along the main highway above the quiet beach road with its tavernas and summer cottages.

From Kiotári a road runs inland to the village of **Asklipió**, nestled in the lee of yet another Knights' castle. Also on the hill above the town is an ancient Greek shrine to Asklepios, the god of healing, which functioned as a therapeutic centre and was staffed by healer-priests. Today Asklipió is

Thárri Monastery is the oldest on Rhodes

one of the most traditional villages on Rhodes, with the odd loaded donkey or working wood-fired oven in the backstreets. The exquisite 11th-century church of **Kímisis Theotókou** (daily 9am–5.30pm; charge) is a beautiful example of Byzantine design located right in the centre of the village. Every nook and cranny of the interior is decorated with rich 15th-century frescoes depicting Old and New Testament scenes in a vividly coloured 'cartoon strip' scheme.

Beyond Kiotári, **Gennádi** is the last major holiday resort on this coast, with conveniently situated accommodation and an endless, clean beach. The centre of the village is picturesque and inhabited nowadays by more immigrant Albanians than native islanders. **Lahaniá**, located 7km (4 miles) south of Gennádi, is an old village partly hidden in a ravine, which has a lovely square with two Ottoman fountains. From both Lahaniá and Gennádi, roads lead to **Plimýri**, a popular if windy sandy cove with a medieval

Remote lighthouse

The lighthouse situated at the far southern tip of the Prassonísi islet used to be staffed, but has been automated since the 1980s, though a keeper still commutes out from Kattaviá to perform maintenance.

chapel and friendly taverna on one side.

Prassonísi, the southernmost point of Rhodes beyond Kattaviá village, has been really opened up to tourism by the paving of the road in; travel time from Líndos is now around 30 minutes non-stop. This is where the Aegean Sea to the northwest meets the Mediterranean Sea to the southeast, so it's almost always windy here, with either the dominant northerlies or rarer southeast wind delighting the windsurfing set, who have two schools (and two sides of the spit) to choose from. Prassonísi used to be a cape linked to the main island, but during 1996 severe storms breached the sandbank, creating a permanent channel between the Aegean and Mediterranean sides and making the cape an islet.

THE WEST COAST

As a rule, Rhodes' western coast is not as stimulating or picturesque as the eastern one. The beaches are not as wide or as sandy, and the prevailing winds and tides carry debris down the Aegean and deposit it directly on the shoreline. However, there are several interesting attractions, and the resort facilities in the northwest – close to Rhodes Town – are among the best on the island.

Ialysos and the Northwest

Diagóras Airport lies on the coast 16km (10 miles) south of Rhodes Town, and there are several villages en route. However, as hotels have multiplied since the 1960s, these separate settlements may appear to have blended into one resort 'strip'. The first resort, **Ixiá**, has the most established tourist area, with several large and luxurious hotels, but was never a village in its own right. Further south, **Triánda**, **Kremastí** and **Paradísi** (by the airport) are villages that have grown due to tourism but still support some Greek domestic activities.

From Triánda or Kremastí it's easy to travel inland to visit the remains of one of ancient Rhodes' most important settlements, **Ialysos**. Unfortunately there is little left of the city-state that was one of a powerful triumvirate with Kameiros and Lindos during the 1st millennium BC – though it was once so extensive that it stretched down the hillside to the coast. The site, on high ground overlooking Rhodes Town, made it a prime strategic position during times of conflict throughout the island's history. It was from here that the Knights consolidated their hold on the island in 1308–9, and also here that Sultan Süleyman had his headquarters during the 1522 siege.

The ruins later became a quarry for stone to build newer towns and structures, including the other main attraction at the site, **Filérimos Monastery**. The monastery has had a chequered life. Revered by Orthodox Christians, it was used as stables

A traditional windmill on the west coast

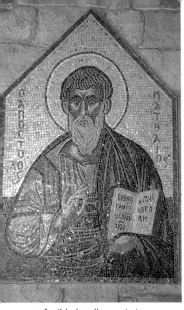

A gilded wall mosaic in Filérimos Monastery

by the Ottomans, renovated by the Italians and bombarded by German forces in September 1943 to dislodge its Italian garrison, before being restored again after World War II. Today, its tranquil dignity shines through, and it's well worth spending a few moments in quiet reflection among the pines. The most impressive building on the site is the 14th-century **Church of Our Lady of Filérimos**, with its rib-vaulted chambers (one built by the Grand Master Pierre d'Aubusson) and small cloister. The mosaic floor in the innermost chapel dates from the 6th century AD, as does a cruciform baptismal font outside, though the stone used was originally part of a Classical temple – illustrating the numerous rebirths of the site.

At the threshold of the church are the remaining foundations of the Classical temples to **Athena Polias** and **Zeus Polieus**. Below these, near the car park, is the entrance to the subterranean Byzantine chapel of **Aï-Giórgis Hostós**, decorated with often faint 14th- and 15th-century frescoes.

Outside the site entrance lies a 4th-century BC **Doric fountain**, which came to light after a landslide in 1926, but is now off-limits again owing to more earth movement. Even if you can't visit the fountain, take a stroll down the pine-shaded avenue with a series of bronze reliefs depicting the

Stations of the Cross, laid out by the Italians. At the end of the lane you reach a huge, nocturnally illuminated **cross** perched atop the 265m (875ft) hillside. The Italians destroyed it in 1941 to deprive Allied airmen of a navigational aid, but it was re-erected to original plans in 1995. It is possible to climb the cross and enjoy panoramic views south over the Italians' hidden airstrip (now a Greek air force base) and north to Sými and Turkey.

The Valley of the Butterflies

South of the airport the developments peter out, though there are occasional beaches signposted right from the main road through grassland or fields. These are quieter than the main resort beaches except at weekends, when local families take a break from town life.

The Butterflies (or Moths) of Rhodes

Petaloúdes is actually a seasonal home not to butterflies but Jersey tiger moths *(Panaxia quadripunctaria)*, which are attracted by the oriental sweet-gum *(Liquidamber orientalis)* trees which grow densely in this valley. Hundreds of thousands of these creatures settle on the tree trunks here between May and September, with peak arrival time during July and August. The moths cannot eat during this final phase of their life cycle, so rest to conserve energy for mating, then die of starvation soon afterwards.

When at rest, the moths are a well-camouflaged black and yellow, but careful examination reveals hundreds resting inconspicuously on the tree trunks. Their Latin name derives from four spots visible when their wings are open, which is augmented by a flash of their cherry-red over-wings when in flight. Though it is tempting to startle the moths into taking to the air by making a sudden loud sound or vibration, this stresses the moths and interferes with their reproduction, so the reserve has strict rules against deliberately disturbing them.

From the main road a left turn leads up into the hills to **Petaloúdes**. This literally translates as 'butterflies', and the area is usually known in English as the **Valley of the Butterflies** (daily May–Sept 9am–6pm, Apr and Oct 9am–5pm; charge varies by season), one of the prettiest spots on the island. The whole valley has been set aside as a well-laid-out reserve for visitors, who can walk through the trees, over streams and around ponds and waterfalls, watching for their first sight of the winged creatures. The climb to the tiny 18th-century chapel of **Kalópetra** at the top of the valley takes about one hour; on the way down there is a snack bar to stop at.

Some 2km (1 mile) downhill from Petaloúdes is the **Micro-winery of Anastasía Triandafýllou** (daily 8.30am–7pm), where you can sample up to 10 varieties of their red, white and rosé bottlings.

The Valley of the Butterflies

The Profítis Ilías Range

The coastal road continues southwest, with the Profítis Ilías range, the island's third-highest, rising inland; a paved side road at Soroní leads towards it. First stop on the north slope of the mountain is strange-looking **Eleoússa**, built in the 1930s as an Italian agricultural colony. On its outskirts sits an enormous Art Deco **fountain-pool**, now

Tiny Ágios Nikólaos Foundouklí

home to captive specimens of the rare local *gizáni* fish, about the size and colour of a guppy. Some 2km (1 mile) west of this stands the tiny Byzantine chapel of **Ágios Nikólaos Foundouklí**. Once part of a larger monastery complex, the four-apsed structure has damp-blurred 13th- to 15th-century frescoes.

The same road from Eleoússa then passes the wooded **Profítis Ilías** peak (798m/2,618ft). Although the summit itself is off-limits owing to military and telecoms facilities, a network of prepared paths through the fragrant conifer forest allows you to explore the lower slopes. From the small **Monastery of Profítis Ilías**, another path descends to Sálakos village just to the north. Beside the monastery is an Italian-built chalet-style hotel which has been restored and returned to service as a boutique hotel.

Kameiros

Beyond Soroní the coast highway threads through seasonally changing farmland until it reaches the turning to the site of ancient Kameiros, just inland. Despite being the smallest, **Kameiros** (Tue–Sun 8am–6.45pm; charge) is the best preserved of Rhodes' three Dorian cities, and it brings to life the daily routine of ordinary people from the Archaic era onwards. Although founded around 1450BC, when Cretans fled their devastated homeland and settled here, the ruins that are visible today date mainly from after 226BC, when most earlier buildings were destroyed by a powerful earthquake.

The ruins cover the hillside in clear urban zones typical of the era. Near the site entrance is the lower **agora**, the main public meeting place, flanked by two temples. Climb the steps ahead of you and turn right to follow the main street trodden by so many ancient sandals, passing numerous small, square rooms to either side; each was a Hellenistic dwelling. Above this residential area, buttressed by a massive retaining wall, lie the remains of a massive **stoa** (covered walkway) 200m (660ft) in length, built in the 3rd century BC. In its time, the shops would have been at the

Kameiros is the best preserved of the three ancient city-states

rear, while an open front supported by a series of double Doric columns allowed the townspeople – and today's visitors – to survey the whole city below them. Beyond the retaining wall's north end yawns a huge **cistern** dating from the 6th century BC, which supplied water to the lower town via a sophisticated system of pipes.

Poppy field

At the town's highest point are the remains of the **Temple of Athena**. There is no Acropolis per se, nor any fortifications, and it seems the peaceable, Minoan-influenced culture and a population largely made up of farmers and craftsmen ensured an unwarlike profile. The rise of Rhodes Town after 408BC resulted in the gradual abandonment of Kameiros. Luckily for modern archaeologists the city was not seen as a great prize to be plundered, only being rediscovered in 1859, and first excavated in 1929. Digs continue, which means that much of the town is off-limits to visitors at any given time.

There are several fish tavernas at **Ágios Minás** beach downhill from ancient Kameiros, though some cater to tourbus clients and can be busy at lunchtime. An alternate lunch spot is **Kámiros Skála** (Kámiros Harbour), 15km (9 miles) further southwest, with its tiny fishing fleet and nets spread on the quay. After lunch you can watch the comings and goings of the daily caiques to the island of Hálki just off the coast. Most days there's a departure at 2.30pm, returning at dawn the next morning, though day-trips are possible on Sunday and Wednesday when boats leave in the morning.

Sunset at Kritinía Castle

Kritinía and Around

As the road climbs away from Kámiros Skála, the ruined **Kritinía Castle** (sometimes called Kastéllo) comes impressively into view on your right. This is one of the delights of southern Rhodes, since the access road is too steep and twisty to allow tour-coach passage, so you will likely only share it with a few other people. The castle was built by the Knights of St John during the 14th century as one of a series of strongholds to protect Rhodes' western coast, in visual contact with their castles on Alimniá islet and Hálki to the west. Its keep is built around the rocky summit, with the curtain walls swooping steeply down; a population of 'Rhodes dragons' – agama lizards – scurry along these and disappear between cracks in the masonry. There is at present no charge or opening schedule, but the vaulted chapel was restored in 2008 and a ticket booth installed at the entrance, so you can expect a working visitor centre or small museum here by 2010.

Kritinía village perches a little way inland from the castle, with its amphitheatrically tiered houses looking out to sea and an atmospheric *kafenío* on the square. The name supposedly derives from the Cretan origins of the inhabitants.

Beyond here the road heads inland to the slopes of Mount Atávyros, at 1,215m (3,949ft) the highest peak on the island, and to **Émbona** village on its north flank, the centre of Rhodian winemaking. During the late summer grape harvest – culminating in an early September local wine festival – the air here takes on a sweet, heavy perfume as the grapes are crushed to produce the must for fermentation. At the edge of Émbona the CAIR and Emery **wineries** both make a range of palatable wines and are open daily in season for tours and tastings (Emery 9.30am–3.30pm); try to visit early or late when there are no coach parties. Wine is also sold from several small storefronts in the village, which despite its evident prosperity and tourist development still has an old quarter of pretty houses bedecked with bougainvillea.

Nearby, sleepy **Ágios Isídoros** is the best starting point for hikes to the summit of **Mount Atávyros**, with the trailhead signposted at the north edge of the village. This barren hump, with just a few giant oaks, could not be more different to Profítis Ilías just a little way north. The round-trip takes about five hours, but you will be rewarded with magnificent views as far as Crete on a clear day. There are also remains of a Bronze Age **Temple to Zeus**, next to a modern radar 'golf ball'.

The spectacular view from Kritinía Castle

The Southwest

Continuing south from Kritinía, the main road veers inland through partly forested mountain scenery. The first village is **Siánna**, famous for producing honey, *soúma (see box below)* and the colourful cotton rugs displayed on every vertical roadside surface.

Soon after the road enters **Monólithos** village, whose older flat-roofed houses around the main church have sweeping views. But there are even better ones 2km (1 mile) west from yet another Knights' castle sitting atop an impressive rocky pinnacle 250m (800ft) above sea level – hence the name Monólithos, meaning 'single rock'. There are great photographic opportunities from the access road and, despite appearances, an easy stair-path leads to the summit. Inside the walls, there is little left of the other castle structures, but a tiny whitewashed chapel adds a typical Greek touch to the image. The paved road continues about 5km (3 miles) to various secluded beaches at **Foúrni**, some of the best on the west coast, though there's only one tiny snack-bar at one cove – the closest proper tavernas are in Monólithos.

South of Monólithos, the broad road passes through Apolakkiá to **Kattaviá**, the southernmost village the island, which gives access to Prassonísi *(see page 62)*. Alternatively, another fast road cuts through the forest from Apolakkiá to Gennádi on the east coast *(see page 61)*.

Village of soúma

Siánna is the only village on Rhodes allowed every autumn to make *soúma*, a distillation of grape pulp, skins and seeds left over after most of the fruit has been pressed for wine. The result, initially about 22 percent alcohol but then concentrated to double that strength, is identical to Italian *grappa*, and in fact the local distilling licence dates from Italian times. Unlabelled bottles of this clear liquid are on sale everywhere in Siánna.

Arriving at Kos Town harbour

EXCURSIONS

As part of the larger Dodecanese archipelago, Rhodes offers opportunities to visit several neighbours, each on a separate day-trip. The catamarans *Dodecanese Express* and *Dodecanese Pride* make it possible to design your own itineraries without signing on to expensive organised excursions. You can also pop over to Marmaris in Turkey, which lies just north of Rhodes' northernmost point.

Kos

A two-and-a-half-hour catamaran trip northwest of Rhodes, Kos ranks second among the Dodecanese in population and size, and has been settled since ancient times, thanks to a good harbour opposite Asia Minor and wide fertile plains. Contemporary Kos is one of the most popular islands with package-holidaymakers, and its many fine beaches, castles and other attractions can be overshadowed after dark by the high-spirited behaviour of some visitors. However, it is easy to steer clear of their excesses by avoiding certain areas and visiting early or late in the season.

Kos Town, near the northeastern tip of the island, has been the main settlement since antiquity, and is a fascinating place to explore. An earthquake in 1933 damaged much of the modern town centre, but allowed Italian archaeologists to expose and excavate a large section of the Roman city directly underneath. Today it is possible to explore the old **agora** (open all day; free), and to walk along Roman roads past exposed patches of mosaics west of the centre, all now a bit lower than the ground level of adjacent modern thoroughfares.

An encounter in the Archaeological Museum

Like Rhodes, the town became a stronghold of the Knights Hospitaller of St John early in the 14th century, and between 1450 and 1514 they built the huge waterfront **Nerantziás Castle** (Apr–Oct Tue–Sun 8am–6pm, Nov–Mar 8.30am–2.30pm; charge) to replace an earlier, flimsier Byzantine fort. The fortification walls make an excellent vantage point for photographs over **Mandráki Harbour** with its excursion boats, while the interior is filled with historical 'debris' such as carved marble plaques, statuary and cannons.

The Knights departed in 1523 without firing a shot, as part of the treaty which surrendered Rhodes (and all the Dodecanese) to the Ottomans. Nearly four centuries of Ottoman rule are attested to just inland from the castle, where the 18th-century **Loggia Mosque**, the largest on Kos, now stands

A mosaic in the Roman agora

silent and closed (though shops occupy its ground floor). There are several smaller mosques scattered across town, a few still used by the small local Muslim population.

Beside the mosque – in fact almost overshadowing it – grows a huge plane tree. Its branches extend so far and its trunk has split into so many sections that for many years it has been supported by a framework of scaffolding. The islanders proudly proclaim this as the **Tree of Hippocrates**, under which the 'Father of Medicine', a native of the island whose bronze statue adorns the harbourfront, would lecture to his students some 2,400 years ago. However, although the tree is certainly one of the oldest in Europe, most experts reckon it to be well under 1,000 years old and therefore not of Hippocrates' era.

The town's main square, **Platía Eleftherías**, is situated 150m/yds inland from the waterfront along pedestrianised Vassiléos Pávlou. The square is surrounded by various fanciful Italian buildings, including the **Archaeological Museum** (Tue–Sun 8.30am–2.30pm; charge), which features excellent Hellenistic and Roman mosaics and statuary, including two portrayals of Kos' favourite son Hippocrates.

At the southern outskirts of the town, on Grigoríou tou Pémptou, lies a Roman **odeion** or small theatre, used in summer for performances. Nearby is the **Casa Romana** (closed for renovations), a 3rd-century AD Roman villa where the mosaic floors show various land and sea creatures.

The **Asklepion** (May–Oct Tue–Sun 8am–6pm, Nov–Apr 8.30am–2.30pm; charge), situated 4km (2½ miles) outside of Kos Town, can be reached by both local buses and a green-and-white, rubber-wheeled 'train' that departs from near the waterfront tourist office. The Asklepion is a religious shrine, spa and therapeutic centre founded shortly after the death of Hippocrates in 370BC. The most conspicuous remains date from the Roman rather than the Hellenistic era, and the site was damaged by the Knights of St John when they removed masonry to build their castle in Kos Town. The main Doric temple to Asklepios, god of healing, stood on the upper level of the three terraces. The site itself was chosen for its mineral-rich spring water – you can still see sections of half-buried clay plumbing feeding the baths – and perhaps also for the fine views across to Turkey.

Hálki

The largest of a group of islands lying a few nautical miles off the west coast of Rhodes, barren, quiet Hálki is the diametric opposite of its larger sibling. It relies on Rhodes for almost everything (except meat from the many sheep and goats), and both the local population and visitor numbers remain relatively low – ensuring an unspoilt atmosphere.

The islanders made a decent living from sponge-diving until the Italians put restrictions on the trade in 1916. This spurred mass emigration to Florida, where natives of Hálki and other Dodecanese islands founded the town of Tarpon Springs and carried on their traditional trade. Hálki slumbered in neglect until the 1980s, when first Unesco and later the conventional tourism companies discovered the island and began to restore many of the handsome houses as accommodation.

Boats dock at the main settlement of **Emborió**, where the lanes are lined by colourful restored mansions. The town is also home to **Ágios Nikólaos** church, with its elegant campanile and, just south, the tallest clock tower in the Dodecanese. On the pedestrianised waterfront, there are several eateries perfect for a leisurely lunch.

West of Emborió, Tarpon Springs Boulevard, the island's first road funded by Floridian émigrés, leads there past the sandy bay of **Póndamos** to the abandoned hillside village of **Horió**, which is deserted except around 15 August when a festival is celebrated at its **Panagía** church. Otherwise Hálki is best explored on foot, or, in midsummer when temperatures climb, by taxi-boats serving remote beaches with poor overland access.

Sunset over the western islands, including Hálki (far left)

Sými

Despite being infertile and waterless, the small island of **Sými** was one of the wealthiest in the Aegean from the 1880s until 1910, prospering from shipbuilding, maritime trading and sponge diving. The shipyard owners, captains and tradesmen built fine mansions and ornate churches. However, the island's fortunes changed when the arrival of steam-powered ships coincided with new Italian restrictions on sponge-gathering. Soon Sými's streets fell silent as most of the workforce emigrated to the US and Australia, leaving the island's grand buildings gradually to crumble away. However, beginning in the early 1980s, first foreign connoisseurs, then rich Athenians, fell in love with this picturesque backwater and snapped up the decaying mansions for restoration as second homes. Like Rhodes Old Town, Sými is protected by the state archaeological service, which ensures that all renovations are done in accordance with traditional architecture and materials.

Perfect Neoclassical mansions overlook Sými Harbour

The small permanent population is more than doubled by expat homeowners and holidaymakers in high season. There are no large resorts on the island, so accommodation is generally in small hotels, apartments or restored houses. The vast majority of people visit Sými as a day-trip from Rhodes, which is about an hour away. Visitors disembark from ships around 10.30am and depart at 4pm. Consequently, the island has two distinct moods – a daytime bustle and relaxed languor in the late afternoons and evening.

Arrival at Sými's major port, **Gialós**, offers one of the most impressive vistas in Greece. Hundreds of Neoclassical stone façades and iron balconies combined with thousands of pastel-hued shutters rise from the harbourside up the slopes. Gialós was always the commercial hub of the island, though now the trade is more likely to be in T-shirts, packaged spices, small trinkets and imported carpets rather than sponges. There are still sponges of all sizes on display, but these are mostly imported from the Caribbean and Asia. Waterfront restaurants entice visitors to stop for a delicious seafood meal, but there is much more to see on the island.

High above Gialós and just out of sight lies **Horió**, the island's inland village, reached either by 357 broad stone steps, the **Kalí Stráta** (the 'Good Road'), or, less strenuously, by bus from the south quay. Horió is crowned by the inevitable Knights' castle, built amid the ruins of Sými's ancient citadel. At the far side of the village is the very worthwhile local **museum** (Tue–Sun 8.30am–2.30pm; charge), highlighting Byzantine and medieval Sými with its displays on some of the island's dozens of frescoed rural churches and an ethnographic collection.

Most day-trips to the island from Rhodes call for

Sými's tribute

When the Knights surrendered the Dodecanese in 1523, the Greek civilian population of Sými, already noted as sponge-divers, sent Sultan Süleyman a placatory gift of the finest sponges for his harem. The Sultan, duly impressed, granted Sými effective autonomy thereafter in exchange for a yearly tribute of sponges, an arrangement honoured until the Italian era.

Panormítis Monastery

about half an hour at **Panormítis Monastery** in the south of the island as part of their itinerary. Unfortunately this means that the monastery can be very crowded if several boats happen to arrive at the same time. In the middle of the compound's pebble-paved courtyard is the church of **Taxiárhis Mihaïl**, with its highly revered icons of the Archangel Michael, patron saint of Dodecanesian sailors.

Marmaris (Turkey)

Although the protracted conflict between Greece and Turkey carried on well into the 20th century, the two nations seem now to be putting the past behind them. Rhodes is very close to Turkey's western coast, so it is possible to enjoy a day (or longer) in this totally different, yet strangely similar, country. You'll need your passport and some small euro or sterling notes for the border control. Although Turkey officially uses the new Turkish lira, almost all transactions can be conducted (at a slight mark-up) in euros or sterling.

The nearest Turkish port to Rhodes is **Marmaris**, an hour away by catamaran. The town occupies the head of a wide bay backed by pine-clad hills that shelter it from north winds – consequently, it is much hotter and more humid in summer than Rhodes. The resort strip, one of the largest in Turkey, dominates the shore just west with a rash of high-rise hotels set behind a coarse-sand beach. East of the centre sprawls a marina with berths for hundreds of yachts.

On a hill in the old quarter is **Marmaris Castle** (sign-posted Müze or museum; daily 8.30am–noon and 1–5.30pm; charge), which offers wonderful views over the bay as well as a small archaeological and ethnographic collection. The climb to the little restored fort, built by Sultan Süleyman, passes the few remaining old houses of the **Kaleiçi** district.

The town's most popular attraction is the *çarşı*, or **bazaar** – a warren of lanes around a tiny hall. Mass-produced trinkets predominate, though there are also spices, leather goods, jewellery, beads, counterfeit designer apparel (often of shoddy quality) including fake pashminas, and discounted 'end of season' clothing. A sense of humour is essential here, as sales tactics are more intense than in Greece, and goods are sold at prices that are not necessarily any cheaper than on Rhodes.

The bustling bazaar at Marmaris

After a spot of retail therapy, shun the fast-food snacks of the bazaar and head down to the easterly waterside for lunch, while watching the distinctive wooden tour *gülets* as they come and go. Many menu items are the same as on Rhodes – only the name changes, and even then not always. This is because Greeks and Turks have lived together, though not always happily, for almost a millennium, and their cultures are more similar than some would like to admit.

WHAT TO DO

Rhodes is not only an excellent holiday destination in terms of ancient sites, museums and historic attractions – it also offers a fabulous range of sporting, shopping and entertainment opportunities. Tour companies also offer excursions, both from resorts to nearby attractions and to other nearby islands.

SPORTS AND OUTDOOR ACTIVITIES

Watersports

There are a huge range of watersports available on Rhodes. Many operators at the popular beaches provide lots of activities for those in search of an adrenalin rush. **Jet skis** are available almost everywhere to rent by the quarter- or half-hour, and there are plenty of **water rides** where you are pulled along by a speedboat in an inflatable ring or banana boat. **Waterskiing** is also on offer at many of the popular bays, including Vlýha. Those who wish to take it one step further and get airborne should head to Faliráki, which has become the **parasailing** capital of the Dodecanese.

With its strong breezes, Rhodes is also one of the best places in Greece to try **windsurfing**. The best locations are wide, fairly shallow sandy bays and where there are no cliffs to disrupt the prevailing winds. Perfect conditions exist at Prassonísi in the far south, a magnet to serious windsurfers. The friendliest place to learn here is Prassonísi Center (tel: 22440 91044, www.prasonisicenter.com). Wind conditions are also good at Ixiá.

Many beaches also have **pedalos** or **kayaks** for hire if you want to try something more sedate.

Shopping for souvenirs in the boutiques of Rhodes Old Town

Local **scuba-diving** outfitters have finally succeeded in expanding the number of permitted areas around Rhodes – the Greek state has always tightly controlled diving owing to the potential for theft of submerged antiquities. The rather dull beginners' area at Pigés Kallithéas lido has now been joined by more exciting, deeper wall-dives at Ladikó and Líndos. The Aegean – or rather, the Mediterranean on the permitted side of the island – is warm and clear, but don't expect a tropical profusion of fish.

At Mandráki quay, two dive operators tout for business in front of their boats; days out (depart 9am, return from site 4pm), including return boat transfer, equipment and two

Best Beaches

Rhodes' beaches come in all shapes and sizes, from tiny coves where you can spend the day alone, to wide sandy bays where you are guaranteed the company of hundreds. The beaches may consist of sand, pebbles or a mixture of the two.

Although many people prefer soft sand over pebbles, when the summer *meltémi* winds blow across the Aegean and cool the west coast (plus more exposed parts of the southeast-facing shore), coin-sized pebbles won't blow around and spoil your day. Pebbles predominate on the coastline around Ixiá, although partly sheltered Élli beach in Rhodes Town is mostly sand. The best sandy beaches line the more protected east coast – broad ones at Faliráki, Afándou, Kálathos and Gennádi, with wonderful small bays at Stegná, Agía Agáthi, Glýstra and Líndos.

On almost all beaches topless sunbathing is accepted, except directly in front of a taverna or within sight of a church. Complete nudism is indulged in at one cove near Líndos, and at very remote bays without facilities between Plimýri and Prassonísi.

The clear, warm water is ideal for swimming

dives (with one tank, however), are frankly pricey at about
€70 – the same amount is charged for the more worthwhile
outings to Ladikó and Líndos.

Reputable dive operators are affiliated with one of two
certifying bodies, sometimes both: PADI (Professional As-
sociation of Diving Instructors) and/or BSAC (British Sub-
Aqua Club). If you're not already a qualified diver, you
can obtain the basic Open Water Diver qualification over
five days of theoretical instruction and practice in a swimming pool, then the sea. 'Try Dive' days are also available
if you're not ready to commit yourself. Waterhoppers (tel:
697 250 0971, www.waterhoppers.com) is the most established diving school.

You can rent or buy **snorkelling** equipment in all the
major resorts, allowing you to explore the shallows. You will
see sea anemones, shoals of fish and even small octopuses
that make their homes in rocky crevices just offshore.

Walking and Hiking

Although there are few pre-pared, marked trails (as opposed to forestry jeep tracks) on the island, the Rhodian landscape offers a seasonally changing experience.

In early spring the hillsides are awash with wild flowers, while later on grain crops give the fields a golden hue. As summer progresses and the crops are harvested (mostly by early July), the terrain becomes drier and dustier. The distinctive trill of the cicada dominates the hottest daylight hours, when no sensible person is out walking. Autumn is perhaps the most pleasant time to be out, even though the days

Following a well-trodden trail near Eptá Pigés

are shorter. Spring and autumn offer the clearest air for panoramic views and photography; a heat-haze rises in summer, reducing long-distance visibility.

Inland, you can hike to the summit of Mount Atávyros from Ágios Isídoros, around the lower slopes of Profítis Ilías from Sálakos, and along the Akramýtis ridge between Siánna and Monólithos, with its wonderful forested scenery. The coastal walk from Faliráki to the Ladikó headland with its coves is a favourite, and there are also hiking possibilities between Tsambíka beach and Haráki. Much the best local walking, however, is on Sými, with paths to remote coves and old chapels, though you'll have to stay there at least two nights to enjoy them. Don't forget to take a supply of water plus snack food, and wear sturdy footwear.

Horse Riding

There are a handful of horse-riding centres on Rhodes. The most established include Kadmos, between Ialysos and Asgoúrou (tel: 694 472 6922, www.rhodesriding.com), with 35 years of experience, and Kentavros (tel: 694 580 2628) behind Tsambíka beach, offering a rather leisurely trip from there to Eptá Pigés and back for about €50.

SHOPPING

The maze-like lanes of the old quarters in Rhodes Town and Líndos host a fascinating mixture of art and ceramics galleries, jewellers, clothing outlets, trinket stalls and out-and-out kitsch displays. Shopping is perhaps the easiest diversion in Rhodes, and the walled city still retains some of the atmosphere of an oriental bazaar. In sharp contrast are the numerous air-conditioned boutiques in the New Town selling brand-name watches, jewellery and designer clothing.

Antiques. For serious collectors there are genuine antiquities (officially classified as anything made before 1821) to be found. These are usually ceramics, jewellery or icons, and will often require authentication certificates and an export permit – the dealer should be able to advise you in this process. For those whose budget or expertise does not

Natural sponges for sale

Locally made ceramic pots are a popular souvenir

stretch to the real thing, there are many reproductions of such items, of varying quality and price.

Ceramics and sculpture. Rhodes still has a thriving ceramics industry, evident in the numerous roadside workshops and retail stores. Plates, jugs and bowls are produced in a bewildering number of patterns and colours. Popular traditional themes include Minoan patterns from Crete, or scenes taken from ancient Greek frescoes or mosaics. Elegant painted house-number tiles make useful souvenirs.

Copies of Classical sculptures are also popular. Prices vary according to the quality of the materials and the skills of the artisan. You will soon discern the variation after visiting a few different stores and closely examining items. In particular, look out for the weight of a piece of pottery or sculpture and the detail in the decoration or carving.

Brass and copperware. Until the 1960s, every household used brass and copper utensils and tools, the copper ones tinned inside for use with food. Since the arrival of stainless-steel ware, electric kitchen appliances and the like, these items – including tureens, ewers, trays, coffee grinders, bowls and *bríkia* (small pots for making coffee) – have found their way to dealers in the Old Town. One worthwhile specialist metal-antiques shop is at Agíou Fanouríou 6 – but the items are not cheap, especially if they are of Ottoman vintage. Light-gauge, lower-quality modern ornamental copper and brass objects are much cheaper and easier to find.

Clothing. Both Rhodes Town and Líndos have plenty of shops with wall-racks festooned with cool cotton or muslin trousers, tops and dresses ideal for summer. You will also find plenty of T-shirts, swimwear and footwear. Umbrellas, especially in Neohóri, are excellent value and come in a myriad of patterns.

Neohóri is also home to an improbable number of designer clothes shops, especially around Platía Kýprou. Storefronts range from British favourites like Marks & Spencer to more upscale brands like Benetton and its Greek imitator Glou. The well-attended August sales coincide with the end of the main tourist season, but you'll have to be quick to find something in your size. The EU is cracking down on cut-rate imitation designer apparel, which is generally found in fly-by-night street stalls, rather than the posh Neohóri boutiques.

Traditional Greek costumes on display

Leather and fur. The Rhodian islanders have always worked the leather from their herds and now make handbags, purses, belts and footwear in a variety of styles and patterns. Specialist boutiques in Rhodes Old Town sell high-quality fur and leather coats and jackets. Pelts are imported with few restrictions, and made-to-measure items can be produced in just a few days.

Carpets. The oriental carpets sold locally are generally imported from Turkey. The indigenous coarse-weave carpet tradition of Rhodes has all but died out; many of the cotton rugs and bathmats on display, with Hellenic motifs such as deer or dolphins framed by a geometric pattern, are mass-produced and imported (usually from India). That said, such mats are cheap, hard-wearing and do not tend to shrink much.

The Genuine Icon

An icon (*ikóna* in Greek) is a religious image of a saint, archangel or apostle, or of a critical event in the life of Christ or the Virgin. They are descended from portraits of the dead on Egyptian mummy sarcophagi at Fayum and are not necessarily meant to be a naturalistic depiction of the holy figure. The visual attributes of each of them – hairstyle, instruments of martyrdom, clothing – were fixed early in Christianity, and do not vary between an ancient or a modern icon.

Icons lie at the heart of Orthodox worship, forming a focus for prayer, and considered a 'window' to the saint being petitioned. All are considered holy, and some are said to possess miraculous powers. The characteristic gold leaf used in their production symbolises the glory of God. The oldest surviving examples date from the latter part of the first millennium.

Icon-painters created works for private clients as well as for churches, and over the years they were popular souvenirs for European Grand Tourists and religious pilgrims. However, modern production methods, including the use of thin canvas and garish synthetic colours, saw them lose favour. In recent years there has been a revival of traditional icon-painting methods, both for church renovations and for commercial sale. Natural pigments and egg tempera (egg yolk and vinegar) binding are painstakingly mixed and applied to a sturdy canvas stretched over wood, or even a solid plank. Gold leaf is then applied, and the whole image is given a patina. Such time-consuming work is exquisite and correspondingly expensive.

Jewellery. You can choose as many carats in precious stones as your budget can handle. Gold and silver are sold by weight, with relatively little extra cost added for the workmanship. Ancient Greek designs – especially Minoan and Macedonian – are very much in evidence. In the lower price ranges there is plenty of everyday jewellery such as ankle chains in metal or leather, navel studs and rings.

Food and drink. Summer fruits – especially sour cherries, figs, plums and bitter oranges – have always been preserved as jars of *glyká koutalioú* or 'spoon sweets'.

Homemade *glyká koutalioú*

Bees frequent the island's aromatic hillside herbs, producing delicious honey to which fresh almonds and walnuts are added. Olives are preserved either in oil or brine, or made into 'extra virgin' (the first pressing) oil for cooking and making delicious salad dressings.

Rhodes has a lower top VAT rate (13 percent) than much of Greece, which makes liquor slightly cheaper than elsewhere in the country. If you want to take a distinctively Greek drink home with you, then try *oúzo* – the best comes from the islands of Sámos and Lésvos. All of the better Greek wines – and there are many – can be found at Marinos (www. marinossa.gr), in suitably cellar-like premises at Ermoú 23 in the Old Town, between the Marine and Arnáldou gates.

Enjoying a quiet drink in Rhodes Old Town

ENTERTAINMENT

Music and Dance

For many, Greek music and dance is inexorably linked to the film *Zorba the Greek*, in which Anthony Quinn performed the *syrtáki* (in fact an amalgam of several different traditional dances) to the sound of the *bouzoúki*, a five-stringed fretted instrument with a haunting effect and a slightly metallic tone.

The rich and varied Greek musical tradition goes back hundreds of years, originally based on Byzantine chant but in modern times featuring wonderful settings of popular poetry to music. Rhythms are very different from those characterising Western music and so can be difficult to follow. Each region of Greece has its own particular songs and dances; those of the southern islands, including Rhodes, are called *nisiótika*.

It is now quite difficult to see genuine dance performances; the best way is at a private wedding or saint's day when the performances occur in their true context (see Calendar of Events on *page 95*). If this is not an option, most large hotels hold regular 'Greek nights', with live music and dancing. While not exactly authentic, they do allow you to get a feel for the passion and movement of Greek dance, and to get into the swing of things by joining in yourself.

If you develop a taste for authentic Greek music, there are two good record shops in Rhodes Town: Sakellaridis, in the Old Town just off Platía Mousíou, with a well-priced collection of quality music in the back (behind the tourist stock) plus vinyl for collectors, or Manuel Music at Amerikís 93 in Neohóri, with a broader choice but higher prices.

Nightlife

The best places for nightlife on the island are Neohóri in Rhodes Town, Líndos and Faliráki, all of which have bars that stay open until around 4am. Hotspots change almost every year, though in Neohóri most of the bars are located on a 150m/yd stretch of Orfanídou. Of these, **Colorado** at Orfanídou 57 has three sound-stages for live acts plus a chill-out bar, and **Sticky Fingers** at Anthoúla Zérvou 6 (a bit south on the hillside) hosts live rock acts several nights a week in high season. At the east end of Élli beach, the Italian-built bathing club hosts a variety of nights from ballroom dancing to Latino disco. The nearby **casino** is the third-largest in the country (Mon–Thur 3pm–6am, Fri noon–Mon 6am continuously; minimum age 23, charge).

Film festival

The Italian-era open-air Rodon cinema in Neohóri hosts an excellent annual film festival in mid- to late June (www.ecofilms.gr). The festival shows feature-length and short films with an environmental theme.

CHILDREN'S RHODES

Rhodes is a great place to take children. Greek society is very family-orientated, and children will be indulged in cafés and restaurants. Most resort hotels have a range of child-friendly activities, including kids' clubs, designated swimming areas and playgrounds.

Since the Mediterranean has very little tide and the island has many gently shelving bays, there are lots of safe places for children to paddle. Sandy beaches are more fun than pebbly ones for castle-building and hole-digging, so bear that in mind when choosing your accommodation.

For older children the watersports on offer at most resorts across the island – pedalos, kayaks, windsurfing – provide an exciting challenge. For a fun day out, try Faliráki Water Park (daily June–Aug 9.30am–7pm, May, Sept–Oct 9.30am–6pm; tel: 22410 84403, www.water-park.gr), with its pools, rivers and a dozen slides.

A trip to the shady Petaloúdes Valley to search for Jersey tiger moths is a great adventure for budding naturalists (see page 66). Kids love riding a donkey from Líndos to its acropolis or even a horse at the Tsambíka riding centre. There are friendly ducks (and somewhat more menacing peacocks) to be seen at the Rodíni Park.

Riding a donkey up to Lindos Acropolis

Gaily painted excursion boats ply between the main resorts and nearby beaches. Children love to watch the coastline go by and spy shoals of fish in the clear water.

Calendar of Events

1 January: *Protohroniá*, or St Basil's Day; the traditional greeting is *Kalí Hroniá*.

6 January: Epiphany; young men dive into the sea to recover a crucifix cast by the local bishop; the retriever is considered lucky for the year.

7 March: Union of the Dodecanese with Greece in 1948 – parades and folk dancing.

Clean Monday: 48 days before Easter, the first day of Lenten fasting (when no meat or cheese may be eaten), marked by kite-flying and outings to the countryside.

25 March: Greek Independence Day/Festival of the Annunciation.

Easter: the most important Orthodox holiday. On Good Friday candlelit processions in each parish follow the flower-decked bier of Christ. The Resurrection Mass at midnight on Holy Saturday is concluded with deafening fireworks and the relaying of the sacred flame from the officiating priests to the parishioners, who carefully take the candles home. On Sunday lambs are roasted, signifying the end of the Lenten fast.

1 May: May Day or *Protomayiá*, marked by flower-gathering excursions to the country – and massive parades by the political Left.

24 June: Birthday of St John the Baptist. On the night before, bonfires are lit and the young leap over them.

15 August: Assumption Day (*Kímisi tis Theotókou*, Dormition of the Virgin, in Greek). Processions and festivals across the island.

8 September: Main pilgrimage day to Tsambíka Monastery and festival at Skiádi Monastery near Mesanagrós, both honouring the Birth of the Virgin.

28 October: *Óhi* (No) Day, commemorating Greek defiance of the Italian invasion of 1940.

8 November: Festival of Archangel Michael at Panormítis, Sými.

December: Carols are sung door-to-door on the evenings of the 12 days of Christmas. On New Year's Eve, adults play cards for money, and a cake (the *vassilópita*) is baked with a coin hidden inside – bringing good luck to whoever gets that slice.

EATING OUT

The backbone of Greek cuisine is local, seasonal ingredients at their peak of flavour and freshness, served raw, or cooked simply – on a grill, flash-fried or slow-baked. Greeks have relied for centuries on staples like olive oil, wild herbs, seafood and lamb or goat's meat, along with an abundance of fresh vegetables, fruit, pulses and nuts, washed down with local wine. The traditional Greek diet is one of the healthiest in the world, and prices in all but the flashest establishments offer reasonable value for money. The prevalence of vegetable and dairy dishes makes eating out a delight for non-meat-eaters.

WHERE TO EAT

On Rhodes you will find a range of eating establishments, often family-run, each type emphasising certain dishes; don't expect elaborate oven-cooked casseroles at a seaside grill, or north European-style desserts at any eatery. However, many island restaurants offer bland fare aimed at the tourist palate; for more authentic cuisine, some of the best eating establishments are listed in the recommendations section *(pages 135–42)*. Some may be in the backstreets away from the pretty views, but the food is superior.

There are several different types of establishment. The *psistaría* offers charcoal-grilled meats, plus a limited selection of salads and *mezédes*. The *tavérna* (written TABEPNA in the Greek alphabet) is a more elaborate eatery, offering the precooked, steam-tray dishes known as *mageireftá*, as well as a few grills and bulk wine.

The *ouzerí* purveys not just the famous aniseed-flavoured alcoholic drink, but also the *mezédes* dishes that complement

A relaxed restaurant with a fantastic view

it – *oúzo* is never drunk on an empty stomach. Octopus, olives, a bit of cheese or a platter of small fried fish are traditional accompaniments, but there are various other hot and cold vegetable and meat dishes to choose from.

The *kafenío* is the Greek coffee shop, traditionally an exclusively male domain, and still so in the Rhodian countryside. Usually very plainly decorated (though tables and chairs are becoming smarter of late), they are the venues for political debate and serious backgammon games. Only drinks – including alcoholic and soft – are served.

WHEN TO EAT

Rhodian resort tavernas open for breakfast, lunch and dinner (many offer a cooked English breakfast). Traditionally, Greeks don't eat breakfast – a coffee and *friganiés* (melba toast) or a baked pastry is about as much as they indulge in. English-style breakfasts are only available in the major resorts and fancier hotels. Lunch is eaten between 2.30 and 4pm, followed by a siesta, before work begins again at around 5.30pm. Dinner is eaten late – usually from 9.30pm onwards, and some establishments will take last orders as late as 12.30am.

If you want to eat earlier, some tavernas begin their evening service at around 6.30pm. You will probably have your choice of table if you eat before 7.30pm, but the atmosphere is definitely better later on when locals come out to eat.

Some tavernas are closed on Sunday evening and part or all of Monday.

WHAT TO EAT

You will usually be given an extensive menu (often in both Greek and English), where items that are available have a price pencilled in beside them. The menu is most useful for checking that the taverna is in your price range (especially for pricey items like meat or fish), whereas a more reliable account of what is available that day can be obtained from your waiter. A good way to familiarise yourself with the various dishes is to order straight from the steam trays or chiller case based on what looks most enticing.

All restaurants render a cover charge. This includes a serving of bread and is usually no more than €1 per person.

Appetisers

Carefully selected, appetisers *(mezédes)* can constitute a full meal in Greece. Shared by the whole table, they are a fun and relaxing way to eat – you simply order as few or as many platters as you want. *Ouzerís* in particular have no qualms about taking orders for *mezédes*-only meals, bringing your choices out on a *dískos* or tray – though they also serve hot main courses.

The most common appetisers are *tzatzíki*, a yogurt dip flavoured with garlic, cucumber and mint; *dolmádes*, vine leaves stuffed with rice and vegetables – sometimes mince – which can be served hot (with *avgolémono* sauce, made of eggs and lemon) or cold (with yogurt); *taramosaláta*, cod-roe paste blended with breadcrumbs, olive oil and lemon juice; *gígandes*, large beans in tomato sauce; *kalamarákia*, deep-fried squid; *mavromátika*, black-eyed peas; *tyrokafterí*, a spicy cheese dip; and *hórta*, boiled wild greens. *Saganáki* is yellow cheese coated in breadcrumbs and then fried, while *féta psití* is feta cheese wrapped in foil with garlic and herbs – often spicy ones – and baked.

Greek salad or *horiátiki saláta* (usually translated as 'village salad') consists of tomato, cucumber, onion, green peppers and olives topped with feta cheese. Cruets of olive oil and wine vinegar are found with other condiments on the table.

A traditional Greek salad

Fish

At fish tavernas you choose from the day's catch, displayed on ice inside a chiller case. This is then weighed, uncleaned, before cooking – check the price as seafood is almost always a relatively expensive option. If the seafood is frozen or farmed (very likely from June to September), this must be stated on the menu – though often rather discretely.

Larger fish are usually grilled and smaller fish fried; all are served with fresh lemon and *ladolémono* (olive oil with lemon juice). Most common species are *barboúni* (red mullet), *xifías* (swordfish), *tsipoúra* (gilt-head bream) and *fangrí* (bream). *Marídes* (picarel), *gávros* (anchovy) and *sardélles* (sardines) are served crisp-fried. More elaborate seafood dishes include *ktapódi krasáto* (octopus in red wine and tomato sauce), *soupiá* (cuttlefish) with spinach-rice, or *garídes* (prawns) in a cheese sauce *(saganáki)*. Fish soup, *psarósoupa*, is most common in the cooler months.

Meat and Casserole Dishes

Meaty snacks include *gýros* (thin slices of pork cut from a vertical skewer and served with tomato, *tzatzíki* and lettuce in pitta bread), or *souvláki* (small chunks of meat cooked on a skewer). Rotisseried chickens, sides of lamb and pork are all cooked to perfection. *Brizóla* – either pork or veal – is a basic cutlet; lamb or goat chops, however, are *païdákia*.

Greece's most famous slow-cooked oven dish is *moussakás* – layers of sliced potato, aubergine and minced lamb topped with a very

Delicious *moussakás*

generous layer of béchamel sauce. It should be firm but succulent, and aromatic with nutmeg. *Pastítsio* is another layered dish with macaroni, meat and cheese sauce. Other common casseroles include *giouvétsi* (meat baked in a clay pot with rice-shaped *kritharáki* pasta) and *stifádo* (braised beef with onions).

For a hot meatless dish, *gemistá* are tomatoes, peppers or aubergine stuffed with herb-flavoured rice; alternatively, *melitzánes imám* (aubergine stuffed richly with tomato, garlic and oil) is reliably vegetarian, as is *briám* or *tourloú* (ratatouille).

Cheeses

Greek cheeses are made from cow's, ewe's or goat's milk, or often blends of two. The best-known cheese is *féta*, popping up in every Greek salad or served alone garnished with olive oil and oregano. *Graviéra* is the most common hard cheese, varying in sharpness; there are also many sweet soft cheeses such as *manoúri* and *anthótyro*.

Favourite fruits

Fruit platters after meals typically feature watermelon or Persian melon in summer, grapes or pears in autumn, sliced apples with cinnamon in winter and citrus fruits or maybe even some luscious strawberries in early spring. Greece imports just a few temperate fruits from Italy or Spain and relatively little tropical fruit, so this is pretty much the full repertoire.

Vineyard at the foot of
Mount Atávyros

Dessert

Most tavernas bring a plate of fresh seasonal fruit *(see box on page 101)* as a finale to your meal. For something more substantial, the *zaharoplastío* (sticky-cake shop) dishes out some of the more enduring legacies of the Ottomans, who introduced some incredibly decadent sweets: *baklavás*, layers of honey-soaked flaky pastry with walnuts; *kataïfi*, shredded wheat filled with chopped almonds and honey; *galaktoboúreko*, custard pie; or *ravaní*, honey-soaked sponge cake. If you prefer dairy desserts, try yogurt with local honey or *ryzógalo*, cold rice pudding at a *galaktopolío* (dairy shop).

WHAT TO DRINK

Greek winemaking goes back at least three millennia; quality, especially at certain mainland vintners, has risen dramatically in recent decades, but owing to limited export – many boutique wineries produce fewer than 20,000 bottles annually – you are unlikely to have heard of even the best labels.

Rhodian wine *(see box opposite)* is more than respectable, served mostly bottled, but also available more cheaply in bulk – *hýma* or *varelísio*. Bulk red, white or rosé are offered in full, half- or quarter-litre measures, either in pink or orange metal cups or glass flagons. Quality varies considerably; if in doubt, order a quarter-litre to start with as a test, plus a can of soda to dilute it.

Retsína has been around since ancient times, when Greeks accidentally discovered the preservative properties of treating wine with pine resin. It complements the olive-oil base of oven-cooked dishes perfectly, but can be an acquired taste and should be served well chilled.

Oúzo is taken as an aperitif with ice and water; a compound in its anise flavouring makes the mixture turn cloudy. Although Rhodes makes its own *oúzo*, the most popular brands come from the islands of Lésvos or Sámos. For a digestif, Metaxa is the most popular brand of Greek-produced brandy, sold (in ascending order of strength) in 3-, 5- and 7-star grades.

Rhodian Wine

Rhodian farmers have always produced wine for domestic consumption, but under the Italians the local wine industry assumed commercial proportions. Today, there are some excellent producers and a good range of labels to choose from. The 1928-founded co-operative CAIR is the major player, but several smaller private wineries such as Triandafyllou below Petaloúdes and Emery or Alexandris in Émbona often exceed it in quality. All can be visited, and their products sampled.

Mass-market CAIR table wines include the dry white Ilios, a red Chevalier de Rhodes, and a basic *retsína*; for a superior label, try their Moulin Sec red or Rodos 2400 white. CAIR also produce several sparkling wines: 10-year-old Brut, Brut and Demi-sec, fermented by both traditional and Charmat methods.

Triandafyllou make some of the best rosé on Rhodes, while recommendable Emery products include their dry white Villaré, or the superior Vounoplagies from *athíri* grapes, currently considered the best white on the island. Their Cava is a heady red, matured in oak barrels. Emery also produce three oak barrel-aged sparkling wines (*méthode champenoise*) in their Grand Prix series.

Everyone's favourite
Greek aperitif

There are nearly a dozen beers produced in Greece (mostly, however, by one brewing conglomerate), as well as imports from Britain, Germany, Belgium and Ireland. Foreign brands made under licence in Greece include Amstel, Kaiser and Heineken. Popular Greek beers include Alfa (reckoned the best), Mythos and Vergina. Rhodes has its very own beer, Magistros, which is micro-brewed in the village of Maritsá.

Non-Alcoholic Drinks

Hot coffee is served *ellinikós* or 'Greek-style', freshly brewed in copper pots and served in small cups. It will automatically arrive *glykós* (sweet) or even *varý glykós* (very sweet) unless you order it *métrios* (medium) or *skétos* (without sugar). Don't drink right to the bottom, as that is where the grounds settle. Instant coffee (called 'Nes' irrespective of brand) has made big inroads in Greece; more appetising is *frappé*, cold instant coffee whipped up in a blender, especially refreshing on a summer's day. If you prefer a proper cappuccino or espresso, there are numerous Italian-style coffee bars.

Soft drinks comes in all the international varieties, while juices are usually from cartons rather than freshly squeezed. Bottled *(enfialoméno)* still mineral water is typically from Crete or the Greek mainland mountains. Souroti is the most widespread domestic sparkling brand.

To Help You Order…

Could we have a table?	**Bouroúme na éhoume éna trapézi?**
Could we order, please?	**Na parangiloúme, parakaló?**
I'm a vegetarian.	**Íme hortofágos.**
Cheers!	**Giámas!**
Bon appetit!	**Kalí órexl!**
Good continuation! (to the next course)	**Kalí synéhia!**
The bill, please.	**To logariazmó, parakaló.**

…and Read the Menu

aláti	salt	**moskhári**	beef
arní	lamb	**neró**	water
avgá	eggs	**oktapódi**	octopus
býra	beer	**pagotó**	ice cream
domátes	tomatoes	**patátes**	potatoes
eliés	olives	**pipéri**	pepper
froúta	fruit	**psári**	fish
gála	milk	**psitó**	roasted
gámberi	big shrimp, prawns	**psomí**	bread
		rýzi	rice
garídes	small shrimp	**revýthia**	chickpeas
		saláta	salad
hirinó	pork	**sáltsa**	sauce
kafés	coffee	**skórdo**	garlic
katsíki	goat	**sta kárvouna**	grilled
kotópoulo	chicken	**sto foúrno**	baked
krasí	wine	**tiganitó**	fried
kréas	meat	**tsaï**	tea
ládi	olive oil	**tyrí**	cheese
lemóni	lemon	**voútyro**	butter
méli	honey	**yaoúrti**	yoghurt
melitzánes	aubergine	**záhari**	sugar

HANDY TRAVEL TIPS

An A–Z Summary of Practical Information

A

ACCOMMODATION

Hotels. Hotels have traditionally been divided into six classes – Luxury, A, B, C, D and E, though a star system (five down to zero) is beginning to replace this. Room rates for all categories other than luxury/five-star are theoretically government-controlled. Ratings are dictated by the common facilities at the hotel, not the quality of the rooms, so a three-star/B-class hotel room may be just as comfortable as a five-star/luxury hotel room, but may not have a conference room, swimming pool or multiple restaurants on the premises.

Many hotels on Rhodes have contracts with European tour operators. This means that in peak season it can be difficult to find desirable accommodation. If you intend to arrive between mid-June and September it is wise to book in advance. At the beginning and end of the season (April–mid-June and October) the island becomes quieter and it is easier to get a good deal. Most hotels close from November to March. In peak season there may be a surcharge if you wish to book for less than three days. Quoted rates should include all applicable taxes.

Pensions, *domátia* and apartments. The main alternatives to hotels are *domátia* (rooms) or full-sized apartments; some of the pensions found in Rhodes Old Town are technically *domátia*. Both licensed rooms and apartments are rated by the tourism authorities from one to three 'keys' based on their facilities. Arrivals by ferry or large catamaran at Kolóna Harbour will be besieged by accommodation touts; it is advisable not to follow them, as only proprietors for the most substandard, unlicensed lodgings resort to this tactic, and you will very likely have to move the next morning.

| I'd like a single/double room with bath/shower | Tha íthela éna monó/dipló domátio me bánio/dous |

AIRPORT

Rhodes' Diagóras Airport is on the west coast of the island, 14km (9 miles) south of Rhodes Town; the **north terminal**, which opened in 2008, is for long-haul international departures only; the adjacent **south terminal** still handles all arrivals and domestic departures, plus a few overseas destinations.

From 6.30am to midnight there is a local bus connection (€2.20) into town. The bus stop is outside between the two terminals (turn left out of arrivals). Otherwise, a taxi into town will cost €17–25 depending on time of day and exact destination.

B

BICYCLE AND MOTORCYCLE HIRE

Cycling is popular during spring and autumn, and in the flatter resorts it is a great way to get around. In Neohóri, both Margaritis at Ioánni Kazoúli 23 (corner of Amarándou) and Bicycle Centre at Gríva 39 rent out a selection of bone-shakers and mountain-bikes.

Hiring a small motorbike is a popular way of cruising the resorts and immediate environs; rates are about €20 per day for a 50cc machine, lower if you hire it for three days or more. However, they're not really suitable for covering long distances on Rhodes, and every year there numerous serious injuries and fatalities involving riders.

It is illegal in Greece to drive any scooter over 50cc without a motorcycle licence, though many unscrupulous agencies ignore this law. If you hire a motorcycle over 50cc without the appropriate licence, any insurance you have will be void if you are injured or involved in an accident.

All riders must wear helmets (a law increasingly enforced, with stiff €175 fines for non-compliance) and should proceed with caution, especially on corners where ground dust and gravel make the road surface slippery.

BUDGETING FOR YOUR TRIP

Rhodes is a moderately expensive destination by European standards
– more than Spain or Portugal, still a bit less than Italy or France.
Flight from Athens: €54–170 (one-way scheduled).
Boat ticket from Athens: €53 (one-way, deck class) to €73 (one-way, cheapest cabin).
Return boat trip to Sými: €30.
Mid-range hotel: €75–130 (one night for two).
Mid-range restaurant: €17–35 (full meal for one).
Admission charges: €2–6 (most museums and archaeological sites).
Car rental: €40 per day, €220 per week (small car in peak season).
Bus fare: ticket prices range from €2–8. Rhodes to Líndos trips
cost €4.50.

C

CAMPING

There are no official campsites on Rhodes and rough camping is
forbidden. However, this does not seem to deter the hundreds of
summertime windsurfers who head down to Prassonísi in their car-
avans and microbuses. With no facilities, this area can become full
of litter by the end of the season.

CAR HIRE (see also Driving)

You will not need a vehicle for Rhodes Town itself, but on the rest of
the island a car allows you to plan your own itinerary and visit sites
at off-peak times of the day. Advance booking online, especially in
peak season when demand is high, makes sense.

   Several major car-hire chains have booths at the airport:
Alamo: tel: 22410 81600; www.alamo.com.
Avis: tel: 22410 82896; www.avis.com.
Hertz: tel: 22410 36702; www.hertz.com.
Sixt: tel: 22410 81995; www.sixt.com.

There are also many reputable local rental agencies that give reasonable service and keener pricing than the major international chains. One especially recommended company with several offices on the island, including at the airport, is **Drive Rent A Car**, tel: 22410 68243, 22410 81011 (airport office), www.driverentacar.gr, the local franchise of international chain Budget.

A national driving licence is accepted for EU/EEA nationals provided that it has been held for one full year and the driver is over 21 years of age. All other nationalities must carry an International Driving Permit in addition to their home licence. You will also need a credit card to avoid paying a large cash deposit upfront.

Many brochure rates can seem alluring because they do not include personal insurance, collision damage waiver (CDW) or VAT (sales tax). Most agencies have a waiver excess of between €400 and €600 – the amount you are responsible for if you smash a vehicle, even with CDW coverage. It is strongly suggested you purchase extra cover (often called Super CDW or Liability Waiver Surcharge) to reduce this risk to zero. If you rent often, consider an annual waiver excess policy from UK-based Insurance4CarHire (www.insurance4carhire.com).

CLIMATE

It is claimed that Rhodes gets 300 sunny days each year – certainly from mid-May until mid-October you are almost guaranteed blue, rain-free skies. Midday temperatures reach a sweltering 38°C (100°F) in the summer months, with hot nights, although evenings become cooler early and late in the season.

The northerly *meltémi* wind that blows down from the Aegean buffets the northwest coast of the island, making it a little cooler throughout the year. The east coast has fewer breezes, and Líndos can be very oppressive on a hot, still summer afternoon.

Considerable rain can fall between November and April, when the air feels damp, although the temperature is seldom especially cold.

CLOTHING

In summer you require very little clothing on Rhodes. Shorts or lightweight trousers and T-shirts or lightweight dresses are fine for sightseeing. Remember to bring comfortable shoes for archaeological sites, as well as a hat and sunglasses. If you have forgotten anything, the boutiques in Neohóri are well stocked (if not especially cheap outside sale periods).

Appropriate dress is compulsory when visiting churches or monasteries. Both sexes should cover their shoulders; men should wear long trousers, and women should wear a skirt that covers their knees.

For evenings, very few places have a dress code, although in smarter hotels men are required to wear long trousers. A light sweater is useful for cooler evenings, especially in early or late season. It can also get remarkably chilly after dark on the decks of ferries, so if you take a day excursion and intend to return late, a jacket or fleece might be a good idea.

CRIME AND SAFETY

Rhodes rates relatively well both in terms of personal safety and the safety of your belongings. Most visitor problems tend to involve motorbike accidents and over-indulgence in sun or alcohol. Serious crime is rare, but it is still prudent to lock any valuables in the hotel safe, and not to leave valuables unsupervised on the beach or on view in your rental car. Don't accept rides from strangers when returning late from clubbing, and always use official taxis.

If you do fall victim to crime, contact the English-speaking Tourist Police, tel: 22410 27423.

CUSTOMS AND ENTRY REQUIREMENTS

EU citizens can visit Greece and its islands for an unlimited amount of time. Irish citizens need some proof of identity, and British citizens must have a valid passport. Citizens of the US, Canada, Australia and New Zealand can stay for up to three months with a valid passport. South African citizens can stay for up to two months with a valid passport. No visas are needed for these stays.

If you wish to extend these timescales you must obtain a permit from the nearest Aliens' Bureau (on Rhodes, a division of the local police), though in practice these have become almost impossible to get for non-EU/EEA nationals.

Greece has typically strict regulations about the import of drugs. All the obvious recreational ones are illegal, and if you are arrested on narcotics charges you can spend up to 18 months on remand before a trial date is set. If you take any prescription painkiller or tranquilliser, carry your supply in the original pharmacy container.

The Greek authorities are very vigilant about the loss of antiquities and national treasures. If you intend to buy an old piece, always deal with a reputable dealer and keep your receipts. Exporting antiquities without a permit is a serious offence.

Since the abolishon of duty-free allowances within the EU, all goods brought into Greece from Britain and Ireland must be duty-paid. In theory there are no limitations to the amount of duty-paid goods that can be brought into the country for personal use. However, cigarettes and most spirits are relatively inexpensive in Greece.

For non-EU citizens, allowances for duty-free goods to be brought into Greece (and Rhodes) are as follows:

200 cigarettes or 50 cigars or 250 grams of tobacco.
1 litre of spirits or 4 litres of wine.
250ml of cologne or 50ml of perfume.

D

DRIVING

Road conditions. Most roads and signs are adequate or better, with the main southeast coast highway widened in 2009–10 from just south of Rhodes Town to Afándou. However, getting to the far south and back in one day can be arduous, and local driving habits leave much to be desired. Since many place-names have been transliterated arbitrarily into Roman lettering and signposted in various different years, you may find the same village name written several different ways as you drive, with only one rendition, perhaps, agreeing with your map. Few parts of the island remain inaccessible to a normal rental car; however, roads have no verges, only dust and gravel along the sides. Many asphalt surfaces are very slick when wet, a problem aggravated by most bends being banked the wrong way to save on culverts.

Rules and regulations. Traffic drives on the right and passes on the left, yielding to vehicles from the right except at roundabouts where one supposedly yields to the left (often countermanded by strange stop-sign schemes). Speed limits on open roads are 90km/h (55mph) and in towns 50km/h (30mph) unless otherwise stated, although most locals do not adhere to the regulations. Both speed-limit and distance signs are in kilometres.

Seat-belt use is compulsory (€175 fine for violations), as are crash helmets when riding a motorcycle (identical fine for non-compliance). Drink-driving laws are strict – expect fines of €400–700 and licence loss if caught – and police checkpoints proliferate at night and weekends. All cars must carry a reflective warning triangle, a fire extinguisher and a first-aid kit; some rental companies may skimp on this. Fines must be paid within 10 calendar days at a post office,

Are we on the right road for…?	Ímaste sto sostó drómo giá…?
Full tank, please.	Óso pérni, parakaló.
super/lead-free/diesel	soúper/amólivdis/dízel
Check the oil/tires/battery.	Na elénxete ta ládia/ta lástiha/ti bataría.
My car has broken down.	I amáxi mou éhi páthi vlávi.
There's been an accident.	Égine éna atýhima.

with proof of payment taken to the designated police station, where your licence may be held to ransom in the meantime.

Rhodes Town in particular is full of one-way systems, which many scooter-riders (and some car-drivers) routinely ignore. Many – especially young army recruits driving military trucks – are inexperienced and may not be properly insured. Give them a wide berth. Pedestrians – especially inebriated holidaymakers – also have their own agenda, and are likely to step out into the roadway without looking.

Parking is tightly controlled in both Rhodes Town and Líndos, where fee schemes apply. The minimum pay-and-display ticket in Rhodes Town is a stiff €1.50, though there are a few free spaces near Élli beach. A new 2009 rule bans parking anywhere along the harbour quay before 10.30am. There is a flat fee of €3 to park in Líndos, though there are free spaces just above the north beach and at Áyios Pávlos bay.

Fuel costs. Prices at the pump are in a state of flux as of writing, varying from €1.10 to €1.30 for all grades of petrol or diesel. Filling stations are reasonably abundant on the coast roads north of Kámiros Skála and Lárdos respectively, but in the south are confined to Kattaviá and Kiotári. They're open daily between the hours of 8am and 7pm (often 8pm in summer).

Breakdowns and accidents. If you have an accident or breakdown, put a red warning triangle some distance behind you to warn on-coming traffic. Always carry the telephone number of your rental office with you; they will be able to advise you if you have difficulties. Almost all agencies subscribe to one or other of the nationwide emergency roadside services (ELPA, Express Service, Ellas Service, Intersalonica); make sure you are given their local numbers.

If you have an accident involving another vehicle, do not admit fault or move either car until the police come out and prepare a report; a copy will be given to you to present to the rental agency. It is an offence to leave the scene of an accident, or move the vehicle before this has been done.

Road signs. Most road signs are the standard pictographs used throughout Europe but you may also see some of these written signs:

ΑΔΙΕΞΟΔΟΣ	No through road/dead end
ΑΠΑΓΟΡΕΥΕΤΑΙ Η ΕΙΣΟΔΟΣ	No entry
ΑΠΑΓΟΡΕΥΕΤΑΙ ΤΟ ΠΑΡΚΙΝ	No parking
ΕΡΓΑ ΕΠΙ ΤΗΣ ΟΔΟΥ	Roadworks in progress
ΚΙΝΔΥΝΟΣ	Danger
ΜΟΝΟΔΡΟΜΟΣ	One-way traffic
ΠΑΡΑΚΑΜΠΤΗΡΙΟΣ ΟΔΟΣ	Temporary detour
ΔΡΟΜΟΣ ΚΛΕΙΣΤΟΣ	Road closed

E

ELECTRICITY

The electric current is 220 volts/50 cycles. Electric plugs are of the Continental two-prong type. Adaptor plugs are available, but it is best to buy one at home before you leave – UK-to-Continental are much harder to find than North-American-to-Continental.

an adaptor	énas metaskhimatistis

EMBASSIES AND CONSULATES

There is an Honorary British Consulate on the island at Grigoríou Lambráki 29, Neohóri, 85100 Rhodes; tel: 22410 22005.

All other national embassies are located in Athens.

Australian Embassy and Consulate: Corner Kifissías and Alexándras avenues, Level 6, Thon Building, 115 23 Ambelókipi; tel: 210 87 04 000, 210 87 04 055 (consulate), www.ausemb.gr.

British Embassy and Consulate: 1 Ploutárhou Street, 106 75 Athens; tel: 210 72 72 600, http://ukingreece.fco.gov.uk/en.

Canadian Embassy: 4 Gennadíou Street, 115 21 Athens; tel: 210 72 73 400.

Irish Embassy: 7 Vassiléos Konstandínou Avenue, 106 74 Athens; tel: 210 72 32 771/2.

New Zealand General Consulate: 76 Kifissías Avenue, 115 26 Ambelókipi; tel: 210 69 24 136.

South African Embassy and Consulate: 60 Kifissías Avenue, 151 25 Maroúsi; tel: 210 61 06 645.

US Embassy and Consulate: 91 Vassilísis Sofías Avenue, 115 21 Athens; tel: 210 72 12 951.

EMERGENCIES

The following emergency numbers are used on the island.

Police: 100	**Ambulance:** 166
Tourist police: 22410 27423	**Fire:** 199
Traffic police: 22410 22346	**Forest fire reporting:** 191

G

GAY AND LESBIAN TRAVELLERS

Greece has historically been a very conservative country where traditional family relationships form the backbone of society. However, there is a natural courtesy towards visitors, and this, combined with the number of different types of international tourists, makes Rhodes a good destination for gay and lesbian travellers. There is a recognised gay nudist beach near Pigés Kallithéas on the rocks well to the left, beyond the Oasis snack-bar.

GETTING THERE

By air. Literally dozens of charter flights carrying package patrons call daily in season from almost every country in Europe, as well as a few from Israel and Turkey; some of those from the UK are available on a flight-only basis.

Currently the only direct scheduled services from Britain are with easyJet (www.easyjet.com) several times weekly in season and Jet2 (www.jet2.com) once weekly from various northern English and Scottish airports.

From North America, you will need to reach Athens first and then continue on one of the three airlines serving the domestic route: Olympic (www.olympicairlines.com), Athens Airways (www.athens airways.com) and Aegean (www.aegeanair.com). Olympic can be the cheapest but is notorious for lateness and cancellations, and faces an uncertain future following its liquidation and reformation as Olympic Air in October 2009. All flights fill quickly in summer – even business class sells out – and must be booked weeks in advance.

Besides Olympic and Aegean, numerous other international carriers fly into Athens. These include Air France: www.airfrance.com, Lufthansa: www.lufthansa.com, KLM: www.klm.com, Swiss: www.swiss.com, and British Airways: www.ba.com.

Direct flights from North America to Athens are provided by Delta Airlines: www.delta.com, Continental Airlines: www.continental.com, and US Air: www.usairways.com.

From Australia and New Zealand there are indirect flights only; the most reliable providers, besides European carriers, are GulfAir: www.gulfairco.com, Singapore Airlines: www.singaporeair.com, Thai Airways: www.thaiair.com, and Emirates: www.emirates.com.

By boat. Rhodes is connected to Piraeus, the port for Athens, by almost daily car and passenger ferry. Sailings are most frequent during school holidays (mid-June to mid-September). Boats can be very crowded at peak times, and it is advisable to buy a ticket as far in advance as possible. Commercial ticket agents in Athens or Piraeus can advise on current schedules and prices.

Of the companies currently providing service, Blue Star, www.bluestarferries.com, is the best. Journey time depends on boat and number of stops: 11 to 12 hours to Piraeus with a Blue Star high-speed craft calling at three or four ports, 15 to 17 hours on a slower, conventional craft, stopping more frequently. There are also links with all the other Dodecanese, and (in summer) the northeast Aegean islands.

From May to October there are also daily catamaran sailings at 4.30pm from Marmaris (Turkey) to Rhodes, plus five weekly from Fethiye (Turkey) to Rhodes at 9am.

GUIDES AND TOURS

Various companies offer organised guided tours to the major sites and attractions. These will be offered at a higher price compared with organising them yourself, but you may find it worth the extra cost for the convenience of being transported by coach.

In Rhodes Town, Triton Holidays (9 Plastíra Street; tel: 22410 21690; www.tritondmc.gr) offer tours, car rental and travel tickets to nearby islands and Turkey, as well as discounted quality accommodation across the Dodecanese.

H

HEALTH AND MEDICAL CARE

Emergency treatment is given free at hospital casualty wards (ask for the *thálamo epigón peristatiká*), but this covers only immediate treatment. EU residents will be able to get further free treatment, but must carry a European Health Insurance Card, obtainable in the UK online or by application to any post office.

Rhodes' main public hospital is 2km (1 mile) south of town, and despite new premises still has a poor reputation. If you are privately insured for medical emergencies, go instead to the well-signed Euromedica clinic in Koskinoú, 6.5km (4 miles) south of Rhodes Town (24hrs; English-speaking staff; tel: 22410 45000).

If you have a minor problem, look for a pharmacy *(farmakío)*, identified by a green cross, where you will be able to obtain basic advice. Most pharmacists will speak some English.

Rhodes has a few scorpions and snakes, which tend only to be found off the beaten track. Mosquitoes, especially in summer, are a more serious nuisance. Topical repellent is useful from dusk onwards; accommodation proprietors often provide insecticide tablets which are vaporised by an electrical device. Spiny sea urchins on submerged rocks can cause injury to inattentive swimmers. Avoidance is the best tactic, but if the worst should happen, dig out the spine tips with a sterilised sewing needle and olive oil.

The sun is strong in Greece; limit your exposure time, apply sunblock regularly and use a hat. Children's skin should always be especially well protected.

Although Rhodes tap water is safe to drink, bottled water often tastes better and is universally available. Always carry water with you to the beach or when sightseeing to protect against dehydration. There are no required vaccinations for Greece.

HOLIDAYS

Official holidays, when most things will be shut, are as follows:

1 January	New Year's Day *(Protohroniá)*
6 January	Epiphany *(Theofánia)*
25 March	Greek Independence Day/Annunciation *(Evan gelismós)*
1 May	May Day *(Protomagiá)*
15 August	Assumption of the Virgin *(Kímisis tis Theotókou)*
28 October	'No' or 'Ohi' Day
25 December	Christmas Day *(Hristoúgenna)*
26 December	*Sýnaxis tis Panagías* (Gathering of the Virgin's Entourage)

Movable official holiday dates include the first day of Lent (Clean Monday; 48 days before Easter Sunday), Good Friday, Easter Monday and Pentecost (Whit Monday, *Ágion Pnévma*; 50 days after Easter Sunday).

L

LANGUAGE

Don't worry if you can't speak Greek. You will find that most people working anywhere near the tourist industry will have a basic English vocabulary, and many speak English very well. You will also find that the *Berlitz Greek Phrase Book and CD* pack covers nearly all of the situations that you are likely to encounter on your travels.

If you want to try your hand at Greek, note that stress is a very important feature of the language, denoted by an accent above the vowel of the syllable to be emphasised. The table below lists the 24 letters of the Greek alphabet in their upper- and lower-case forms, followed by the closest individual or combined letters to which they correspond in English.

A	α	a	as in *father*
B	β	v	as in English
Γ	γ	g	as in *go* (except pronounced 'y' before 'e' and 'i')
Δ	δ	d	like **th** in *this*
E	ε	e	as in *get*
Z	ζ	z	as in English
H	η	i	as in *ski*
Θ	θ	th	like **th** in *thin*
I	ι	i	like **ee** in *meet*
K	κ	k	as in English
Λ	λ	l	as in English
M	μ	m	as in English
N	ν	n	as in English
Ξ	ξ	x	as in *box*
O	ο	o	as in *toad*
Π	π	p	as in English

P	ρ	r	as in English
Σ	σ/ς	s	as in English, except sounds like **z** before m or g sounds
T	τ	t	as in English
Y	υ	y	as in *country*
Φ	φ	f	as in English
X	χ	h	as in Scottish *lo**ch***
Ψ	ψ	ps	as in *ti**ps**y*
Ω	ω	o	as in *b**o**ne*

MAPS

You'll find a range of free maps at hotels, the airport and car-rental offices, all with advertising. These are adequate for exploring the attractions of the Old Town, though not precise enough to pinpoint attractions on smaller side streets.

Most maps of Rhodes and the surrounding islands are out-of-date or inaccurate; the Road Edition 'Rhodes' 1:100,000 map is one of the best commercial maps available.

MEDIA

Newspapers. You will be able to buy all the major European newspapers, including the Paris-based *International Herald Tribune*, which appears daily and includes the English-language version of top local paper *Kathimerini* (www.ekathimerini.com). The *Athens News* (www.athensnews.gr) is published every Friday and has plenty of events listings and a TV guide. *IHT/Kathimerini* also have a competing higher-quality weekly, *Athens Plus*, every Friday.

Television. Most hotels of three stars and above have a range of satellite channels, including CNN and BBC World. The Greek state channels ET1 and NET often have foreign films in the original language, especially late at night.

MONEY

Currency. Greece uses the euro (abbreviated €), with notes of 5, 10, 20, 50, 100, 200, 100 and 500 euros; each euro comprises 100 cents and coins have denominations of 1, 2, 5, 10, 20 and 50 cents plus 1 and 2 euros.

Currency exchange. Most banks operate currency exchange for foreign notes and travellers' cheques (you'll need proof of identity for the latter); they charge a percentage commission for the service of between 1 and 3 percent and queues are long, so you may prefer to obtain cash from an ATM. Exchange rates, the same everywhere, are usually posted on a noticeboard inside the bank or in the window.

ATMs. There are ATMs in all the major resort areas, and at least one in the larger settlements inland. These accept just about any type of debit card – look for your card's logo above the machine. Despite commissions of up to 3 percent levied by your home bank, this is usually the most convenient and quickest way to get cash – although queues develop during high season, and machines can run out of notes at weekends.

Credit cards. Many hotels, restaurants, travel agencies and shops accept credit cards, but there is still a sizeable minority that do not. Some may charge 3–5 percent extra for credit card payments, to cover their bank charges. It is always advisable to ask about credit card acceptance before you sign the register or order your food, to avoid difficulties later.

I want to change some pounds/dollars.	**Thélo na alláxo merikés líres/meriká dollária.**
How much commission do you take?	**Póso promýthia pérnete?**
Can I pay with this credit card?	**Boró na pliróso me avtí tin pistotikí kárta?**

O

OPENING TIMES

Opening hours differ for official organisations and privately owned businesses. They also vary significantly between high and low season. To be sure of service or admission, it is best to visit any establishment between 9am and 1pm.

Banks operate Mon–Thur 8am–2.30pm, Fri 8am–2pm.

Most museums are open Tue–Sun 8.30am–3pm (this will vary). Most archaeological sites are open throughout the day and are closed on Mondays in winter. The last admission is usually 20 minutes before the official closing time.

Smaller shops are open Mon–Sat 9am–2.30pm, plus Tue, Thur and Fri 5.30pm–9pm; supermarkets are open 8.30am–9pm Mon–Fri, 8.30am–8pm Sat. A few (especially ones in the main resorts) may also open on Sunday. In peak season shops selling tourist-related items may stay open until quite late.

P

POLICE

Ordinary police wear a two-tone blue uniform; the traffic police *(trohéa)* are part of the force. The tourist police is another branch that deals with tourist problems and complaints. They speak English and wear a dark grey uniform.

Emergency: 100
Non-emergency: 22410 23849
Tourist police: 22410 27423
Traffic police: 22410 22346

Where's the nearest
police station?

Pou íne to kondinótero
astynomikió tmíma?

POST OFFICES

Post offices can be identified by a bright yellow-and-blue Hermes head and the initials ELTA. They are generally open from 7.30am–2pm. The main Neohóri post office is open Mon–Fri 7.30am–8pm and Sat 8.30am–2pm. Post offices also have franchises of Western Union Moneygram.

Stamps can be bought here, or at kiosks and newsagents for a small premium. The standard price for sending a postcard to an overseas destination is €0.70.

A stamp for this letter/ postcard, please.   Éna grammatósimo giaftó to grámma/kart postál, parakaló.

PUBLIC TRANSPORT

Bus. The bus network links all the major settlements on the island with Rhodes Town and operates from early in the morning until 7–10pm depending on the destination. Photocopied timetables are available from tourist information offices, or just consult the placards at the stops. Buses for the east side of the island depart from the Papágou end of Odós Avérof, by the New Market; for the west side and the airport, buses depart from 50m/yds further up Odós Avérof street, also outside the New Market.

Taxis. The island is well equipped with taxis, which are dark blue and white on top. Prices to all destinations are regulated and posted outside the arrivals terminal at the airport, as well as being detailed on a sheet issued by the Tourism Directorate – though this does not entirely prevent fare-fiddling with foreigners, which can be brutal.

The basic charge structure also appears on a laminated sheet mounted on the dashboard. Meters must be set at the start of each journey; '1' indicates regular fare, '2' indicates double tariff between midnight and 5am, and/or outside urban areas.

If your hotel calls a taxi for you (small extra charge for appointment), the receptionist will give you the taxi number. Some extra long or short journeys are unpopular with drivers, who may refuse to take you. Additionally, most taxi drivers refuse to enter the walled Old Town – resign yourself to walking in from the nearest gate.

Ferries. There are regular commercial ferry services from Rhodes to all of the Dodecanese islands, as well as Crete, some of the Cyclades and all of the northeast Aegean islands, plus connections to Piraeus and Thessaloníki on the Greek mainland. The main passenger port is at Kolóna Harbour, and numerous ticket agents can arrange your passage.

R

RELIGION

Most of the population belongs to the Greek Orthodox Church. There are several Roman Catholic churches and a synagogue in Rhodes Town, as well as two active mosques. Details of Catholic masses are posted outside both San Francisco/Ágios Frangískos (by Ágios Athanásios Gate) and Santa Maria della Vittoria/ Panayía tís Níkis (in Neohóri), which is also used by some Protestant denominations.

T

TELEPHONES

The international code for Greece is 30. All land-line numbers in Rhodes have 10 digits. Numbers in the north begin with 22410, while those in the south start with 22440. Greek mobile numbers begin with 6 and, like land lines, have 10 digits.

Card-operated telephone booths are numerous, but rather than use calling cards issued by OTE (the Greek telecoms entity), most people use prepaid calling cards (in €5 and €10 denominations) with free access numbers prefixed 807 (reachable from any call box or private phone) and a 12-digit PIN. Savings are typically around 70–80 percent compared with OTE standard rates, and similar to using Skype or other VOIP programmes to call a land line. Most hotels have direct-dial facilities but charge ruinously for calls; usually the circuitry permits use of the prepaid discount cards from your room phone.

Mobile users will be able to roam on any of three local networks, but again charges are steep. If you are going to be around more than a week, it is worth buying a Greek SIM. Your own phone can be unblocked if necessary at any computer shop, for a small fee.

TIME ZONES

Greece is two hours ahead of Greenwich Mean Time and also observes Daylight Saving Time – moving the clocks one hour forward at 3am on the last Sunday in March, one hour back at 3am on the last Sunday in October.

New York	London	Jo'burg	Rhodes	Sydney	Auckland
5am	10am	11am	noon	7pm	9pm

TIPPING

Service is included in restaurant and bar bills, although it is customary to leave any small change on the table for the waiting staff, and large parties should leave 5–10 percent of the total bill.

Taxi drivers are not tipped per se except at Easter week, but collect €0.32 per bag in the boot, plus various surcharges for entering the airport (€2.15) or harbour (€0.86).

Hotel chambermaids should be left a tip of around €2 per day. Bellhops and doormen should be tipped up to €2, depending on services provided.

Toilet attendants should be left around €0.30.

TOURIST INFORMATION

The moderately helpful Dodecanesian Tourism Directorate, part of the Greek National Tourism Organisation, tel: 2241 935 226, www.ando.gr/eot, is found at the corner of Papágou and Makaríou in Neohóri (Mon–Fri 8.30am–2.45pm). The Municipal Tourist Office is nearby on Rimini Square by the main taxi stand, tel: 22410 35945 (June–Oct Mon–Sat 8am–9.30pm, Sun 9am–3pm).

For tourist information before you travel to Greece, contact one of the GNTO's following overseas offices:

Australia and New Zealand: 51–75 Pitt Street, Sydney, New South Wales 2000, Australia, tel: (2) 92411663, e-mail: ehto@tpg.com.au.

Canada: 91 Scollard Street, 2nd Floor, Toronto, Ontario M5R 1GR, tel: (416) 968 2220, e-mail: gnto.tor@sympatico.ca.

UK and Ireland: 4 Conduit Street, London W1R 0DJ, tel: (020) 7495 4300, e-mail: eot-greektouristoffice@btinternet.com.

US: Olympic Tower, 645 Fifth Avenue, New York, NY 10022, tel: (212) 421 5777; 168 North Michigan Ave, Suite 600, Chicago IL 60601, tel: (312) 782 1084; 611 West Sixth St, Suite 2198, Los Angeles, CA 92668, tel: (213) 626 6696; e-mail: info@greektourism.com.

W

WEBSITES AND INTERNET ACCESS

There are just a handful of useful websites dedicated to Rhodes, most of them establishment-driven:

www.rodos.com allows you to book accommodation or car hire and visit resorts virtually

www.rhodes.gr is the municipality's site, but is not kept up to date

www.rhodesguide.com has useful guides to the resorts and beaches

www.rhodesliving.com is of most interest to resident expats

The better hotels have wi-fi zones (usually for a fee) or ethernet cables in the rooms; internet cafés are fairly abundant in places like Faliráki, Líndos and Rhodes Town, but tend to have a short life-span.

Recommended Hotels

The following recommendations include options for all budgets and cover Rhodes Town's old and new districts and the rest of the island, as well as some popular excursion destinations.

Most resort-type hotels on Rhodes have several different types of room, including suites and bungalows, so be sure to confirm the type of accommodation that you are booking. Most hotels of three stars and over will have wi-fi available in the rooms or lobby (often for a fee).

Unless otherwise indicated, accommodation operates only from April to October. Accommodation prices can vary significantly between high and low season. Tax and service charges should be included in quoted rates, though breakfast (typically €6–12 per person) may not be.

Almost all hotels take credit cards (we indicate 'cash only' where this is not the case), especially if they are bookable through their websites. The price categories indicated below are for a double room per night in high season.

€€€€€	over 250 euros
€€€€	150–250 euros
€€€	100–150 euros
€€	60–100 euros
€	below 60 euros

RHODES OLD TOWN

Andreas €€ *Omírou 28D, 851 00 Rhodes, tel: 22410 34156, www.hotelandreas.com.* At the quietest, highest point of the Old Town stands this exquisite little hotel (officially a pension) with comfortable rooms in a variety of formats, from tiny singles and family quads to a spectacular tower suite in what was a Turkish mansion. All units are air-conditioned, though some bathrooms are down the hall. The multilingual, multinational staff's attentive care and welcoming smiles mean that guests often come for two nights (the minimum period) and stay for a week or more – if busy bookings permit. Their terrace bar, which has free wi-fi and great views, is an excellent location for breakfasts (extra) and evening drinks. Open Mar–Dec.

Apollo Tourist House €€ *Omírou 28C, 851 00 Rhodes, tel: 22410 32003, www.apollo-touristhouse.com.* The 'house' comprises six different wood-panelled pastel-hued doubles, with raised bed platforms and bed curtains. The best unit is the galleried north-facing one. Congenial English-Japanese management; breakfast is in the secluded courtyard with splashes of the traditional ochre and powder-blue Ottoman wall colouring. Normally open Apr–Oct.

Avalon €€€€€ *Háritos 9, 851 00 Rhodes, tel: 22410 31438, www.avalonrhodes.gr.* This 14th-century manor house, converted in 2007 with no expense spared, contains six luxury suites (some are suitable for families or groups, four have original fireplaces) with state-of-the-art bathrooms, plasma TV and internet connection. Breakfast is served in your suite, or down in the vaulted bar. Rack rates can top €500 per night but internet specials may make it more affordable. Open all year.

Marco Polo Mansion €€€ *Agíou Fanouríou 42, 851 00 Rhodes, tel: 22410 25562, www.marcopolomansion.gr.* Hardly noticeable off the cobbled thoroughfare, this discreet inn, converted from a rambling old Ottoman mansion (the hamam survives, though it is not in use), is stunning once inside. All en suite rooms are furnished with antiques from the nearby eponymous gallery, plus natural-fibre, handmade bedding; the garden-side rooms are a bit cheaper (but also less airy). Buffet breakfasts are served in the courtyard with its well, which becomes one of Rhodes Town's best restaurants after dark. Open mid-Apr–Oct.

Niki's Rooms € *Sofokléous 39, 851 00 Rhodes, tel: 22410 25115, www.nikishotel.gr.* Set in the south central Old Town, this is an excellent budget pension with a helpful owner. Some of the plain rooms are smallish, but all are en suite, many are air-conditioned, and three of the top-floor rooms have private balconies (otherwise there are two communal terraces, as well as a washing machine and fridge for guests). Open Apr–Nov.

Spot € *Perikléous 21, 851 00 Rhodes, tel: 22410 34737, www.spot hotelrhodes.com.* Although housed in one of the Old Town's few modern buildings, the cheerful, air-conditioned rooms here represent good value. The buffet breakfast (extra charge) is served on the rear patio. Other bonuses include a roof terrace, on-site internet café, wi-fi, luggage storage and the knowledgeable Greek-American proprietor. Open Mar–Nov. Cash only.

Via-Via €€ *Lysipoú 2, alley off Pythagóra, 851 00 Rhodes, tel: 22410 77027, www.hotel-via-via.com.* Efficiently run small hotel, with tastefully decorated rooms, mostly en suite and air-conditioned. All are simply but tastefully furnished with bedding and textiles in subdued colours. Three grades of breakfast are offered, and there are fantastic views of the mosque dome opposite from the roof terrace. Open all year.

RHODES NEW TOWN

Cactus €€ *Kó 14, 851 00 Rhodes, tel: 22410 26100, www.cactus-hotel.gr.* Three-star hotel of 1970s vintage, partially renovated in 2006, with a pool – though you are opposite the best, northern end of Élli beach. Rooms are fair-sized if unexciting, with large, white-tile bathrooms; the co-managed Aquarium (www.aquarium-hotel.gr) across the way has more rooms facing the square rather than the sea but shares the same decor, down to the plexiglas balcony barriers.

Esperia €€ *Gríva 7, 851 00 Rhodes, tel: 22410 23941, www.esperia-hotels.gr.* Another three-star hotel in a quiet corner of Neo-hóri, overlooking a little plaza. Rooms aren't enormous, but are tasteful and pastel-hued, with showers rather than tubs in the bathrooms, and a pool. Open all year.

Mediterranean €€€ *Kó 35, 851 00 Rhodes, tel: 22410 24661, www.mediterranean.gr.* Flanking one of the livelier parts of Élli beach, with its own sun loungers, the enduringly popular Mediter-

ranean was refurbished in 2000 and is set for further phased renovation in coming years. Facilities include a full-service restaurant,
busy café and freshwater pool. Open all year.

Rodos Park Suites Hotel €€€€ *Ríga Fereoú 12, 851 00 Rhodes,
tel: 22410 24612, www.rodospark.gr.* Arguably the best-quality
accommodation in the New Town (yet very convenient for the
walled city), this small boutique hotel, renovated in 2008, offers
three grades of rooms and suites with sleek modern fittings. Rear
units face a quiet hillside, front ones overlook the fair-sized pool.
The basement 'wellness spa' and two on-site restaurants complete
the picture. Open all year.

AROUND THE ISLAND

Atrium Palace €€€€–€€€€€ *Kálathos beach, 851 02 Rhodes, tel:
22440 31601, www.atrium.gr.* This unobtrusive, family-friendly
'thalasso spa resort' occupies vast, attractively landscaped grounds
extending down to the beach, with several novelty pools, mini-golf,
tennis courts and several restaurants. Even the standard doubles
have large bathrooms and parquet floors, while the luxury villas
down near the spa are the quietest.

Elafos €€ *Profítis Ilías, 851 00 Rhodes, tel: 22460 22402, www.
elafoshotel.gr.* After languishing neglected for decades, this Italian-
built period piece from 1929 reopened in 2006 as a boutique hotel.
The high-ceilinged units (the three suites are worth the extra
charge) have considerable retro charm, and there are great views
of the forest from the balconies. The à la carte ground-floor restaurant makes a good rest stop if touring. Open all year (there is a
sauna for winter).

Esperos Palace €€€ *Faliráki, 851 00 Rhodes, tel: 22410 84300,
www.esperia-hotels.gr.* While perhaps overrated as a five-star
(adults only) resort, understated good taste is evident here from
the white-and-beige lobby to four grades of futuristic rooms and
suites with their subtle lighting, flat-screen TVs and miniature
sound systems. Bathrooms, with separate WC, are functional but

small at the most basic 'Select' grade. Common areas, merging with those of the co-run Esperides Palace 'family' resort adjacent, include several pools set in mature gardens, a gym, sauna-spa and a good stretch of beach.

Lindian Village €€€€€ *851 09 Lárdos, tel: 22440 35900, www. lindianvillage.gr.* This ingeniously designed bungalow complex just beyond Glýstra cove has its own private beach, a small spa/gym, several gourmet restaurants and three grades of units (the suites have their own secluded plunge-pools). Although children are accommodated, it is really more of a romantic adults' resort.

Lindos Mare Hotel €€€€ *Vlýha, 851 07 Rhodes, tel: 22440 31130, www.lindosmare.gr.* Situated on a hillside just 2km (1 mile) northwest of Líndos, this tiered hotel manages to feel low-key and intimate despite comprising 142 designer units (one-third suites; not all of them with sea views). A funicular (or shady walkway) brings you down through lush grounds from the larger of two pools to the beach, with just sun loungers – no watersports. There are also two full-service restaurants and a fully equipped spa. Immediately adjacent, the ultra-sleek adults-only **Lindos Blu €€€€€** *(tel: 22440 32110, wwww.lindosblu.gr)* is a five-star annexe, inaugurated in late 2008, a bit forbidding by comparison until the landscaping grows in.

Melenos €€€€€ *851 07 Líndos, Rhodes, tel: 22440 32222, www. melenoslindos.com.* Built fairly recently in traditional style, this boutique hotel has taken advantage of the best location in the village. The 12 wood-trimmed units vary in plan, but all have big designer baths with glazed Kütahya tiles, and semi-private sea-view patios with pebble mosaics underfoot. Whether it is worth the €270–800 per night price tag is a personal matter. There is an equally pricey bar-restaurant sheltering under a fabric marquee with stunning views.

Miramare Wonderland €€€€€ *Ialysoú Avenue, Ixiá, 851 00 Rhodes, tel: 22410 96251, www.blue.gr.* Beautifully designed deluxe hotel of suites and bungalows in several grades, set in lawn-gardens behind the beach in Ixiá, 3.5km (2 miles) from Rhodes Town. Facilities include pools for both children and adults, two restaurants, three bars, a fitness centre, watersports and children's club. A 19th-century English mining train carries guests around the vast site.

Paraktio Apartments €€ *Kiotári, 851 00 Rhodes, tel: 22440 47278, www.paraktio.com.* Exceptionally well-appointed studios for couples and galleried four-person apartments with huge terraces, perched on a bluff just above a nice stretch of beach. The units are fully self-catering, but there is a small snack-and-breakfast bar on site. Friendly family management, no package bookings.

Rodos Palace €€€€ *Triandón Avenue, Ixiá, 85 100 Rhodes, tel: 22410 25222, www.rodos-palace.com.* As much a business and conference hotel as a five-star resort, the Rodos Palace offers five grades of accommodation. These range from standard rooms and executive suites in the ugly junta-era main tower to the three types of suites in prettier two- or three-storey villas in a landscaped hillside setting through which an artificial 'lazy river' runs – really the best reason to stay here. All have minimalist, light-tone furnishings; some have private plunge pools. The centrepiece of the vast common areas is a greenhouse-domed pool, best in winter; watersports are offered across the road at the beach.

KOS

Afendoulis €€ *Evrypýlou 1, 853 00 Kos, tel: 22420 25321, www. afendoulishotel.com.* The friendliest place to stay in Kos Town, the Zíkas family hotel has large air-conditioned rooms with balconies, and a loyal repeat clientele – so advance booking is necessary. No frills, but wi-fi and internet access, and breakfast available long hours in the lobby or on the shady patio. Open 15 Mar–15 Nov.

Grecotel Kos Imperial Thalasso €€€€ *Psalídi district, 853 00 Kos, tel: 22420 58000, www.grecotel.com.* Among 10 or so hotels in this resort strip a few kilometres east of town, this is doubtless the most luxurious and most stunningly designed. The mixture of standard doubles and bungalows in lushly landscaped grounds share most features (including small balconies) and are priced more according to view. One of several pools has a 'tropical waterfall' and 'lazy river' feature, while the spa is (as the name suggests) sea water-based. Open Apr–Oct.

SÝMI

Aliki €€€€ *Aktí Gennimáta, Gialós, 856 00 Sými, tel: 22410 71665, www.hotelaliki.gr.* This 1895 mansion right on the quay was tastefully converted into one of Sými's most exclusive hotels during the 1990s. The tasteful rooms all have wooden floors and antique furnishings, although only some have sea views and/or balconies (at a price premium). An affiliated seafood restaurant is located next door. Apr–Nov.

Iapetos Village €€€ *Behind Gialós Platía, 856 00 Sými, tel: 22460 72777, www.iapetos-village.gr.* A complex of spacious, balconied maisonettes and studios that is unique, not only for its covered swimming pool (the only one on Sými), but for luxuriantly landscaped grounds complete with palm trees and other exotics. A good breakfast is offered either in the cool basement or by the pool bar, or you can prepare your own in the well-equipped kitchens. Open Apr–Nov.

HÁLKI

The Captain's House € *Emboriós, 851 10 Hálki, tel: 22460 45201.* On an island where independent accommodation is hard to find, this 19th-century mansion converted to an en suite inn is among the best options. There are no sea views, but it is quietly situated with a lovely front garden, and English-speaking hosts Alex and Christine Sakellarídis are welcoming. It is often booked weeks in advance. Cash only.

Hiona Art €€€ *South quay, Emboriós, 851 10 Hálki, tel: 22460 45244, www.hionaart.gr.* After a decidely chequered career, the municipally run hotel housed in an old sponge factory emerged from a total overhaul in 2008 as a boutique lodging with its own lido, gym and conference facilities. Reserve well in advance, as special-interest groups often book it.

Recommended Restaurants

The following recommendations range from authentic local *ouzerís* and traditional tavernas to some of the most renowned restaurants on Rhodes. Most restaurants open for lunch and dinner daily unless otherwise noted. The majority do not take reservations, but where this is recommended it is noted in the description. Larger restaurants are now required to have a non-smoking section, but eating outside is often the only effective solution.

Credit cards are not universally accepted – we have indicated the last known policy – so double-check before you order. Prices indicated are per person without wine.

€€€€€	over 50 euros
€€€€	37–50 euros
€€€	27–37 euros
€€	20–27 euros
€	below 20 euros

RHODES OLD TOWN

Mandala €€ *Sofokléous 38, tel: 22410 38119.* Popular garden bistro-café serving generic Mediterranean salads, stews and pasta dishes; that said, the young Greek clientele come as much for the crowd and the buzz as the food. After hours it becomes more of a bar, with good beer, a woodstove inside for winter and occasional live acoustic music at weekends. Open 11am–3am summer, from 7pm only Oct–Apr except Sun 1–7pm. Cash only.

Marco Polo Café €€ *Agíou Fanouríou 42, tel: 22410 25562.* The courtyard of the Marco Polo Mansion is the setting for some of the Old Town's most creative cooking. Platters change seasonally but might include subtly flavoured pilaf with lamb and raisins, or pork medallions with soft *manoúri* cheese, fig and red peppercorn sauce. Decadent desserts include chocolate frozen with strawberries, lemon-yoghurt or white-chocolate mousse and *kaltsoúnia* (sweet turnovers). Co-proprietor Spýros is a wine fanatic, so you can dip into his cellar if the bulk wine fails to appeal. Open mid-May to mid-October supper only; last orders 11pm. Major credit cards.

Mikes €€ *Alley behind Sokrátous 17, tel: 22410 23855.* This galley-like diner (the name is pronounced 'mee-kess') has just a few tables in the lane and serves some of the freshest and least expensive seafood on the island. Not much else other than surprisingly elaborate salads and wine. Open Apr–Nov. Cash only.

Myrovolies €€€ *Láhitos 13, off Sokrátous, tel: 22410 38693.* There is limited seating on the patio or in the old interior of this popular 'cosy' *ouzerí* – best on cooler evenings as it can get quite stuffy otherwise – so arrive early for a good seat. The emphasis is on hearty pork and mushroom-based dishes, with bottled wine only. Live music three nights a week. Open all year for supper, closed Mon–Tue winter. Cash only.

Nireas €€€€ *Sofokléous 22, tel: 22410 21703.* Atmospheric indoor/outdoor seating under vines or stone arches makes this a good choice for a romantic supper or a last-night blowout. Food is fresh fish and shellfish – including smooth Venus clams, limpets, mussels and miniature Sými shrimps – followed by Italian desserts like panna cotta and tiramisu. Open Apr–Nov. Major credit cards.

Romios €€ *Sofokléous 15, tel: 22410 25549.* There is something for everyone (especially vegetarians) at this popular taverna that looks touristy but delivers the goods: unusual *mezédes* like *bourékia kaïsariótiko* (turnovers stuffed with *pastourmás* and *anthótyro*), aubergine recipes, pizza, traditional *magireftá*, hearty meat platters, a few seafood offerings, decadent desserts and a well-priced wine list. Hot *mezédes* come in little iron skillets. Seating is on the square or in the cosy interior. Closed Dec to late Mar. Credit cards.

Sea Star €€–€€€ *Sofokléous 24, tel: 22410 22117.* This inexpensive yet quality seafood outlet offers a limited menu of scaly fish, shellfish and starters like *kápari* (pickled capers) and *koliós pastós* (salt-cured mackerel). Seating is indoors in the cooler months (not open midwinter), otherwise outside on the little square. Cash only.

La Varka €€ *Sofokléous 5, tel: 22410 75688.* Seafood-strong *ouzerí* with much sought-after outside seating, plus a pointed-stone, wood-ceilinged interior. The menu includes good salads, *pikilíes* (medley platters) for two, grilled *thrápsalo* (big deep-water squid), fish soup with whole fish on the side, fried or salt-cured seafood titbits, a reasonably priced wine list and Siánna *soúma* by the carafe. Open daily summer 11.30am–2am, winter Wed–Sun evenings. Cash only.

RHODES NEW TOWN

Ammoyiali €€€€ *Voríou Ipírou 17, corner of Kennedy, tel: 22410 23980.* Probably the most visually stunning restaurant interior on Rhodes – Far East-themed, as one of the owners is a t'ai chi instructor – plus an outside wood deck for balmy evenings. The menu – unusual preliminary nibbles, Med-fusion starters, meat and fish mains – is very nearly as good and fairly priced, though the wine list considerably inflates bills. Dinner daily, lunch high season only. Major credit cards.

Anatolikes Nostimies €€€€ *Klavdíou Pépper 109, Zéfyros beach, tel: 22410 29516.* The name translates as 'Anatolian Delicacies': Middle Eastern dips and starters, plus a preponderance of beef-based kebabs rather than the usual lamb or pork – the owners are Muslims from Greek Thrace. Beach-hut atmosphere, but friendly, popular, and there is post-prandial hookah on request. Daily noon–midnight. Cash only.

Marasia €€ *Platía Agíou Ioánnou 155, southwest of Áyios Athanásios Gate, tel: 693 258 6983.* Seafood-strong *ouzerí* operating in the courtyard and interior of a 1923-vintage house adorned with old photos. Plenty for vegetarians – aubergine turnovers, grilled oyster mushrooms, stuffed squash blossoms – plus platters like butter-flied *savrídi* (horse mackerel), snails, cuttlefish in wine and herring salad, as well as a full meat-grills list. Rhodian bulk and bottled wine list along with *oúzo* to drink. Open all year. Visa.

Meltemi €€ *Platía Koundourióti 8, Élli beach, tel: 22410 30480.* Classy and surprisingly well-priced *ouzerí* offering such delights as crayfish nuggets, octopus croquettes, grilled red peppers in balsamic vinegar, chunky *húmmus* and superb roast aubergine with beans and onions to a local crowd. There is a pleasant winter salon with old engravings inside. Open all day, all year. Cash only.

Paragadi €€€€ *Corner of Klavdíou Pépper and Avstralías, Zéfyros, tel: 22410 37775.* Seafood restaurant where reasonable prices for wine and a limited range of vegetarian starters is offset by somewhat bumped-up fish prices; their seafood risotto is excellent, though it won't satisfy purists. Sea views during the day; large parties must book weekend nights. Closed Sun evening and (usually) Mon noon. Credit cards.

Sakis €€ *Kanadá 95, corner of Apostólou Papaïoánnou, Zéfyros, tel: 22410 21537.* A friendly old favourite with pleasant patio and indoor seating, equally popular with Rhodians and foreigners. Known for its shellfish (such as limpets, mussels and snails), meat (chops, Cypriot *sheftaliés*) and the usual starters. Daily all year 5pm–1am, also Sun lunch. Cash only.

Steki tou Tsima €€ *Peloponníssou 22, 200m/yds south of Kókkini Pórta, tel: 22410 74390.* Sympathetic seafood taverna with only fresh, seasonal fish, shellfish like *foúskes*, *strídhia* (oysters) and cuttlefish grilled with their own ink, excellent chips, and a limited range of vegetarian starters, accompanied by a large assortment of well-priced *oúzo*, scoffed by a largely local clientele. Very convenient after taking in a movie at the two nearby multiplexes. Open nightly except Sunday midday only. Cash only.

Steno € *Ayíon Anaryíron 29, 400m/yds southwest of Áyios Athanásios Gate, tel: 22410 35914.* Long-running, cult *ouzerí* with indoor/outdoor seating according to season, attracting a mix of locals, ex-pats and some savvy tourists (including visiting dignitaries). The proprietor, Ilías, is from Kárpathos, something reflected in a menu encompassing chunky sausages, *pitaroúdia* (courgette-based croquettes), *hórta* (stewed greens), chickpeas, beans, stuffed squash flowers, green beans with garlic and simple seafood platters. Daily all year, supper only. Cash only.

Thavma en Kairo €€€€ *Eleftheríou Venizélou 16–18, tel: 22410 39805.* People come to this Swedish-run restaurant as much for the location in this elegant Belle Époque mansion and the jazz soundtrack as for the food, which is mainly Med-Greek seafood with an Asian twist. Vast (and pricey) selection of beers, wines and cocktails; service can be slow. Open most of the year from 7pm Mon–Sat. Major credit cards.

AROUND THE ISLAND

Koutouki € *Maritsá village centre, no phone.* Out in the central uplands is the little village of Maritsá, whose pedestrianised main street supports seven tavernas of all pretensions. The simplest – and one of the best, near the top of the hill – is this always-packed dive (what *koutoúki* means), where for a set low price you eat whatever half-dozen platters chef Ioánnis Vélis – moonlighting from his day job at the airport – decides to serve. This might be chicken fillet in cumin, spare ribs, assorted pulses, lamb or salads. People bring their own fish to be cooked, and some bachelors eat here every day. Open all year except Sundays. Cash only.

Maria € *Access road to Tsambíka beach, tel: 693 929 3280.* Presiding over the grill, Kyra Maria is the heart and soul of the most bucolic of a trio of tavernas in the olive groves and grazing goats here. Seating is under a shelter or out on the thick lawn, with a playground for kids. The menu includes chunky *tyrokafterí*, fried whole peppers, hand-cut chips and a selection of meats or *magireftá*. Open all day. Cash only.

Mavrikos €€€ *Main taxi square, Líndos, tel: 22440 31232.* This family-run restaurant, in business since 1933, is rated by locals and visitors alike as among the best on the island for its extensive menu of exquisite oven-cooked dishes and seafood (with less prominent meat dishes). *Gígandes* in carob syrup, sweet marinated sardines, or beetroot in goat-cheese sauce precede fishy mains like skate timbale with sweetened balsamic vinegar, or superior interpretations of old standards such as *dolmádes* or *tyrokafterí*. Excellent (and expensive) Greek wine list. Open Apr–Nov. Major credit cards.

Oasis € *Kallithéa shoreline, no phone.* This deceptively simple-looking *kantína*, a friendly one-woman operation, is much the best of several local snack-bars, each dominating its own patch of cove amidst the rock formations. The menu, like the gravel-floor decor, is simple but wholesome: salads with pickled capers and *peperoncini*, grilled or fried seafood platter and *kolokythókeftedes* (courgette croquettes). Other bonuses include beer in iced steins and great views south towards Cape Ladikó. Open Apr–Oct. Cash only.

Palios Monolithos €€ *Opposite the church, Monólithos Village, tel: 22460 61276.* A favourite weekend lunch venue that serves well-cooked grills, several dishes of the day, unusual starters like wild mushrooms or mixed-leaf *dolmádes* and superior (homemade) wine. It has indoor/outdoor seating (and a distant sea view), and there is always a warm welcome from owners Manólis and Déspina. Open all year, weekends only off-season. Major credit cards.

Pelecanos €€ *Bypass road, Váti, tel: 22440 61100.* Sleek 2008-inaugurated taverna which is best at weekends when it fills up and the full menu is guaranteed. A wide range of salads, good thick cheese pie amongst other *orektiká* and succulent meat grills. There is beer and *oúzo* for those wishing to steer clear of the stiffly priced wine list. Open all year (winter weekends only); cash only.

Perigiali €€ *Near the fishing anchorage, Stegná, tel: 22440 23444.* Locals come to eat on this raised, tree-studded patio for the excellent seafood, savoury, hand-cut round chips, homemade *yaprákia* (stuffed vine leaves) and copious salads ('Perigiali' has caper greens and grilled aubergine) washed down by good bulk wine. The travertine-clad loos are certainly unique on Rhodes. Open Apr–Nov. Cash only.

Pigi Fasouli €€ *Psínthos, tel: 22410 50071.* A good meal stop if touring inland Rhodes. Vegetable starters include chunky aubergine salad and beets with their greens, or expertly fried vegetable slices with *skordaliá*, but expect mostly goat in various guises, a few meat-based casserole dishes, or simply grilled lamb chops. You have to ask if you want to try the owner's own, off-menu bulk wine. Sadly, there is no seating by the *pigí* (spring) of the name, but the outside terrace overlooks the shady oasis here. Open Apr–Oct 9am–10pm, Nov–Mar weekends only. Cash only.

Platanos € *Lower platía, Lahaniá Village, tel: 22440 46027*. The most attractive village-centre seating on Rhodes, bar none, under the plane trees after which the restaurant is named, beside two gushing Ottoman fountains. The indoor premises are housed in a sumptuous new building. The mezédes *(dolmádes, húmmus, kopanistí)* are top-notch, as are the mains, though fish here is as pricey as elsewhere. Open all year (weekends only winter). Cash only.

Plimiri Beach €€ *Near Zöodóhou Pigís church, Plimýri Bay, no phone*. Operating out of the grounds of a late-medieval church, this ever-popular fish taverna is well placed for lunch on a driving tour of the island. Presentation (and to some extent prices) is 1980s-style, with excellent chips and a few starters accompanying a wide selection of fresh fish. Open Apr–Oct noon until late. Cash only.

Stegna/Kozas €€–€€€ *Stegná coast road, north end, tel: 22440 22632*. Founded in 1932 and now in its third generation of management, this somewhat pricey but excellent, friendly seafood taverna is worth it for such delights as village bread with olive paste, chunky aubergine salad with pine nuts and sweet red peppers, and *soupiá stín meláni* (cuttlefish in its own ink), as well as shellfish and scaly fish. A wide range of beers comes in iced mugs; retractable glazing on the water-level terrace permits year-round operation. Cash only.

KOS

Ambavris € *Ambávris hamlet, 800m (½ mile) south of Casa Romana in Kos Town, tel: 22420 25696*. One of the best-value tavernas on the island, with lovely courtyard seating. Opt for the *mezédes* medley and enjoy such Koan delicacies as *pinigoúri* (bulgur pilaf), *pikhtí* (brawn), spicy *loukánika* (sausages), *fáva* bean purée and stuffed squash blossoms. Open May–Oct, supper only. Cash only.

Ouzeri Limni (Karmolengos) € *Linopótis junction for Pýli, tel: 22420 41579*. At lunchtime the noise from the adjacent highway can distract, but after dark it is well worth driving out here for a variety of dishes, from *atherína* (sand smelt) and fresh *bakaliáros* (hake) to baked chickpeas and grills, served in three portion sizes to suit any appetite. There is also an excellent range of *oúzo*, *tsikoudhiá* (the Cretan spirit) and *tsípouro* (the mainland variant) on offer. Open all year Wed–Mon noon–11pm. Cash only.

SÝMI

Mythos Mezé €€€ *South quay, Gialós, tel: 22460 71488.* Supper-only terrace venue on the roof of the former summer cinema, serving some of the most imaginative cooking on the island. Chef-owner Stavros' generous tasting menu features *psaronéfri* (pork medallions) with mushrooms and sweet wine sauce, lamb *stifádo*, feta *saganáki* in fig sauce and desserts like lemon pie or panna cotta. An annexe near the bus stop, **Mythos Fish**, stresses à la carte seafood. Booking required for both premises (same telephone number). Mythos Mezé open late May–late Sept; Mythos Fish open Apr–Nov lunch and dinner (supper only spring/autumn). Major credit cards.

Syllogos €€ *Just south of Platía Syllógou, Horió, tel: 22460 72138.* Cavernous but not impersonal place with indoor/outdoor seating, great for taverna standards like *skordaliá*, *arní lemonáto*, fried fish and aubergine *imám*, with good Rhodian bulk wine – though portion sizes could be more generous. Open Apr–Nov. Cash only.

HÁLKI

Remezzo € *Emboriós quay, tel: 22460 45010.* The best spot on the island for pizzas and top-notch *magireftá* (cooked casserole dishes). Open Apr–Oct. Cash only.

Tou Vangeli €€ *Ftenágia Lido, tel: 694 599 8333.* While most restaurants line the harbourside, a 10-minute walk south will bring you to this gravel lido and its adjacent taverna. Seafood mains and *mezédes* are excellent, though it's wise to confirm the price of *oúzo* carafes in advance. Cash only.

INDEX

Berlitz pocket guide

Rhodes

Sixth Edition 2010
Written by Lindsay Bennett
Revised by Marc Dubin
Edited by Anna Tyler
Series Editor: Tony Halliday

Printed in Singapore by Insight Print
Services (Pte) Ltd, 38 Joo Koon Road,
Singapore 628990. Tel: (65) 6865-160
Fax: (65) 6861-6438

Berlitz Trademark Reg. U.S. Patent Of
and other countries. Marca Registrada